CITY MAZES

REAL STREET MAP PUZZLES TO SOLVE
FROM AMSTERDAM TO VANCOUVER

Published in March 2018 by Lonely Planet Global Limited
CRN 554153
www.lonelyplanet.com
ISBN 978 1 78701 341 4
© 2018 Quarto Publishing PLC
Printed in China
10 9 8 7 6 5 4 3 2 1

The book was conceived, designed, and produced by
Quintet, an imprint of The Quarto Group
58 West Street
Brighton
BN1 2RA
United Kingdom

Quintet, an imprint of the Quarto Group:
Publisher Mark Searle
Editorial Director Emma Bastow
In-house Editor Leah Feltham
Project Editors Lyndsay Kaubi, Katie Crous
Designers Luke Herriot, Ginny Zeal, Michelle Rowlandson
Illustrators Racket
Puzzle designer Patricia Moffett

Lonely Planet:
Publishing Director Piers Pickard
Associate Publisher Robin Barton
Editor Christina Webb
Art Director Daniel Di Paolo

STAY IN TOUCH lonelyplanet.com/contact

AUSTRALIA The Malt Store, Level 3, 551 Swanston St,
Carlton, Victoria 3053 T: 03 8379 8000
IRELAND Unit E, Digital Court, The Digital Hub,
Rainsford St, Dublin 8
USA 124 Linden St, Oakland, CA 94607
T: 510 250 6400
UNITED KINGDOM 240 Blackfriars Rd, London SE1 8NW
T: 020 3771 5100

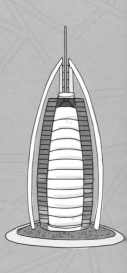

CONTENTS

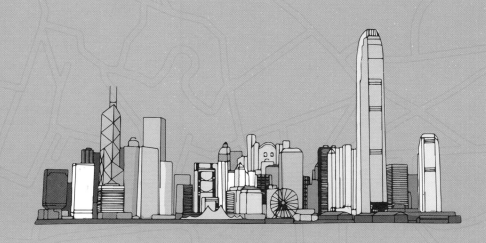

INTRODUCTION

The cities of the world – whether they're modern, steeped in tradition, developing or all three – are premier destinations for all types of travellers. In this book, some of the world's most distinctive, intriguing and outstanding cities have been turned into challenging mazes for the armchair traveller and adventurous puzzle enthusiast alike.

This book features a total of 30 cities, each of which has staked its rightful place on an increasingly competitive and crowded world stage. As an intrepid puzzle-solver, you are tasked with finding your way from start to finish, enjoying an insightful tour as you go. Each maze is based on the real street map for the relevant city, give or take the odd liberty. Wind your way through backstreets, stride down main thoroughfares and negotiate expansive parks and meandering rivers to explore your possible route.

As you explore the maps, you'll discover the sights and experiences of each city, ranging from major landmarks and tourist hotspots to hidden gems and quirky local hideouts. Read all about them in the accompanying descriptions.

So, pack your pencil and eraser, and journey to the metropolis of your choice. Take in the sights, sounds, smells and tastes of the urban landscapes on offer as you tackle the challenge of the book's 30 mazes.

How to use this book

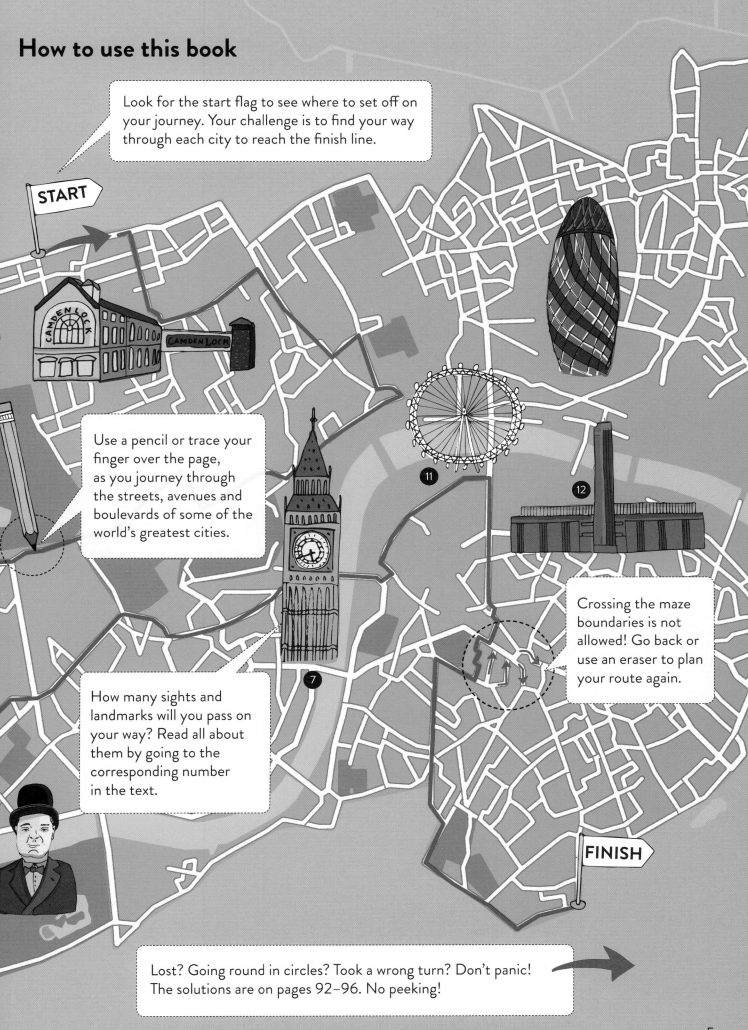

Look for the start flag to see where to set off on your journey. Your challenge is to find your way through each city to reach the finish line.

START

Use a pencil or trace your finger over the page, as you journey through the streets, avenues and boulevards of some of the world's greatest cities.

How many sights and landmarks will you pass on your way? Read all about them by going to the corresponding number in the text.

Crossing the maze boundaries is not allowed! Go back or use an eraser to plan your route again.

FINISH

Lost? Going round in circles? Took a wrong turn? Don't panic! The solutions are on pages 92–96. No peeking!

SAN FRANCISCO

You're just as likely to find yourself as you are your way around the chilled yet vibrant San Francisco streets. Leave your inhibitions at home and dive into good times as you make your way from east to west.

PACIFIC HEIGHTS

PRESIDIO HEIGHTS

RICHMOND

HAIGHT-ASHBURY

THE CASTRO

FINISH

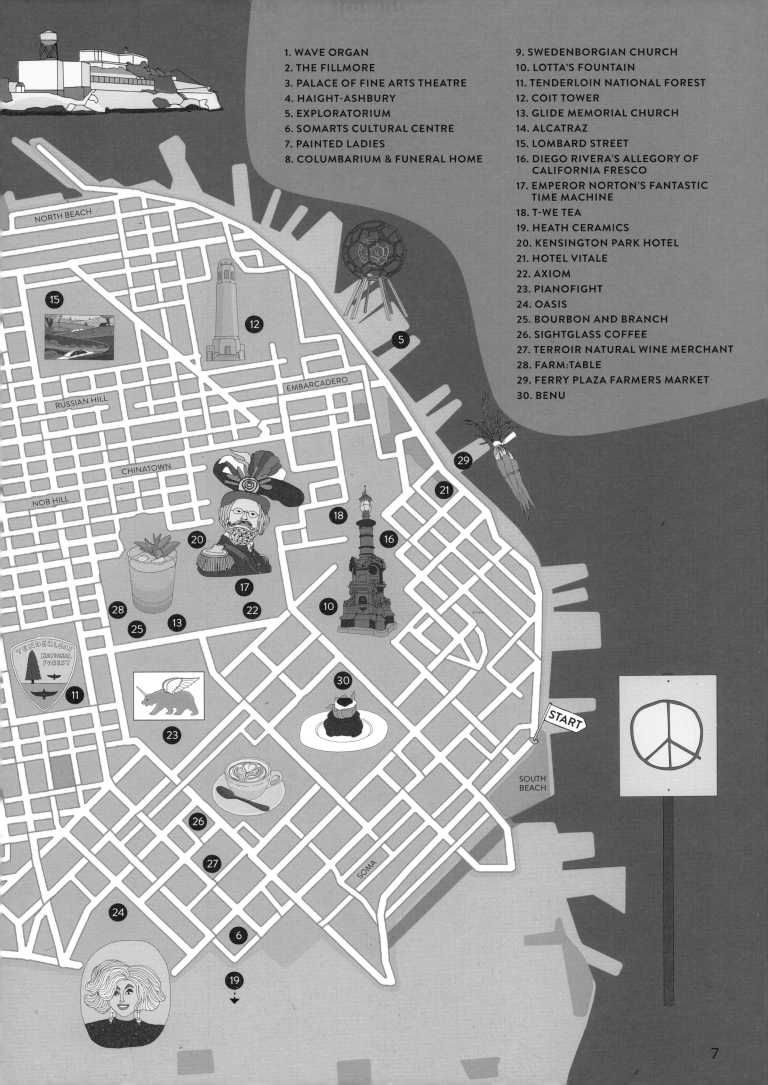

1. WAVE ORGAN
2. THE FILLMORE
3. PALACE OF FINE ARTS THEATRE
4. HAIGHT-ASHBURY
5. EXPLORATORIUM
6. SOMARTS CULTURAL CENTRE
7. PAINTED LADIES
8. COLUMBARIUM & FUNERAL HOME
9. SWEDENBORGIAN CHURCH
10. LOTTA'S FOUNTAIN
11. TENDERLOIN NATIONAL FOREST
12. COIT TOWER
13. GLIDE MEMORIAL CHURCH
14. ALCATRAZ
15. LOMBARD STREET
16. DIEGO RIVERA'S ALLEGORY OF CALIFORNIA FRESCO
17. EMPEROR NORTON'S FANTASTIC TIME MACHINE
18. T-WE TEA
19. HEATH CERAMICS
20. KENSINGTON PARK HOTEL
21. HOTEL VITALE
22. AXIOM
23. PIANOFIGHT
24. OASIS
25. BOURBON AND BRANCH
26. SIGHTGLASS COFFEE
27. TERROIR NATURAL WINE MERCHANT
28. FARM:TABLE
29. FERRY PLAZA FARMERS MARKET
30. BENU

NORTH BEACH

RUSSIAN HILL

CHINATOWN

NOB HILL

TENDERLOIN NATIONAL FOREST

EMBARCADERO

START

SOUTH BEACH

SOMA

SAN FRANCISCO

If there's a skateboard move yet to be busted, a technology still unimagined or a poem left unspoken, chances are it's about to happen in San Francisco. Look up and you'll notice crooked Victorian rooflines, wind-sculpted treetops and fog tumbling over the Golden Gate Bridge. Good times and social revolutions tend to start here, from manic gold rushes to blissful hippie be-ins.

1 WAVE ORGAN

The Wave Organ is a sound sculpture of PVC tubes and concrete pipes capped with marble from San Francisco's old cemetery. Depending on the waves, winds and tide, the tones emitted sound like nervous humming from a dinnertime line cook or spooky heavy breathing over the phone in a slasher film.

2 THE FILLMORE

Jimi Hendrix, Janis Joplin, The Doors – they all played the Fillmore. Now you might catch the Indigo Girls, Willie Nelson or Tracy Chapman in the historic 1250-capacity, standing-room-only theatre (if you're polite and lead with the hip, you might squeeze up to the stage).

3 PALACE OF FINE ARTS THEATRE

Like a fossilised party favour, this romantic, ersatz Greco-Roman ruin is the city's memento from the 1915 Panama-Pacific International Exposition. A glorious spot to wander day or night.

4 HAIGHT-ASHBURY

This legendary intersection with its eye-catching store fronts was the epicentre of the psychedelic '60s, and 'Hashbury' remains a counterculture magnet. On average Saturdays here you can sign Green Party petitions, commission a poem and hear Hare Krishna on keyboards and Bob Dylan covers on banjo.

5 EXPLORATORIUM

Is there a science to skateboarding? Do toilets really flush anticlockwise in Australia? Find out things you'll wish you learned in school at San Francisco's thrilling hands-on science museum.

6 SOMARTS CULTURAL CENTRE

All roads in San Francisco's art underground lead to this nonprofit creative community hub under a highway overpass. Shows have featured eviction letters turned into art, Mike Arcega's restatement of Emma Lazarus' 'Statue of Liberty' poem with found objects, and Sean Anomie's long-exposure photos of car taillights.

7 PAINTED LADIES

Hippie communes and Victorian bordellos, jazz greats and opera stars, earthquakes and Church of Satan services: these genteel 'Painted Lady' Victorian mansions have hosted them all since 1857, and survived elegantly intact.

8 COLUMBARIUM AND FUNERAL HOME

Art-nouveau stained-glass windows and a dome skylight illuminate more than 8000 niches honouring dearly departed San Franciscans and their beloved pets. San Francisco's Columbarium revived the ancient Roman custom of sheltering cremated remains in 1898, when burial grounds crowded the Richmond district.

9 SWEDENBORGIAN CHURCH

Radical ideals in the form of distinctive buildings make beloved SF landmarks; this standout 1894 example is the collaborative effort of 19th-century Bay Area progressive thinkers, such as naturalist John Muir, California Arts and Crafts leader Bernard Maybeck and architect Arthur Page Brown.

10 LOTTA'S FOUNTAIN

In 1875 Lotta Crabtree, a diminutive opera diva, donated this cast-metal spigot fountain (thrice her size) to San Francisco. During the April 18, 1906 earthquake and fire it became downtown's sole water source.

11 TENDERLOIN NATIONAL FOREST

www.luggagestoregallery.org/tnf

Dead-end Cohen Alley has been transformed by a nonprofit artists' collective: a grove of trees is taking root, walls are covered with murals, and mosaic pathways and koi ponds have replaced the asphalt.

12 COIT TOWER

www.sfrecpark.org/destination/telegraph-hill-pioneer-park/coit-tower

The exclamation mark on San Francisco's skyline is Coit Tower, with 360-degree views of downtown and wrap-around 1930s murals glorifying workers; take the elevator up to the tower's open-air platform.

13 GLIDE MEMORIAL CHURCH
www.glide.org

When the rainbow-robed Glide gospel choir enters singing their hearts out, the 2000-plus congregation erupts in cheers, hugs and dance moves. Raucous Sunday Glide celebrations capture San Francisco at its most welcoming and uplifting.

14 ALCATRAZ
www.nps.gov/alcatraz

Alcatraz: for over 150 years, the name has given the innocent chills and the guilty cold sweats. Over the decades, the island has been a military prison, forbidding maximum-security penitentiary and disputed territory.

15 LOMBARD STREET

The tourist board has dubbed this 'the world's crookedest street', which is factually incorrect, but Lombard is scenic, with its red-brick pavement and lovingly tended flowerbeds.

16 DIEGO RIVERA'S ALLEGORY OF CALIFORNIA FRESCO
www.sfcityguides.org/desc.html?tour=96

Hidden inside San Francisco's Stock Exchange tower is a priceless art treasure: Diego Rivera's 1930–31 *Allegory of California* fresco, spanning a two-storey stairwell.

17 EMPEROR NORTON'S FANTASTIC TIME MACHINE
www.emperornortontour.com

Travel through time on this tour with San Francisco's self-appointed Emperor Norton (aka historian Joseph Amster) across two miles of the most dastardly, scheming, urban-legendary terrain on Earth.

18 T-WE TEA
www.t-wetea.com

Start your day the SF way in this speciality boutique with a T-We tea to match your attitude: sprawl in Dolores Park with the Hipsters in Wonderland blend or huddle like Sunset surfers over Foggy Morning Brekkie.

19 HEATH CERAMICS
www.heathceramics.com

Odds are your favourite SF meal was served on Heath Ceramics, Bay Area chefs' tableware of choice. Heath's muted colours and streamlined, mid-century designs stay true to Edith Heath's originals c1948.

20 KENSINGTON PARK HOTEL
www.kensingtonparkhotel.com

Arrive at the dramatic 1925 Spanish lobby to check in to your dashingly handsome guestroom, blending Moorish patterns, Victorian flourishes and contemporary dark-wood furnishings.

21 HOTEL VITALE
www.hotelvitale.com

When your love interest or executive recruiter books you into the waterfront Vitale, you know it's serious. The office-tower exterior disguises a snazzy hotel with sleek, up-to-the-minute luxuries.

22 AXIOM
www.axiomhotel.com

Of all the downtown hotels aiming for high-tech appeal, this one gets it right. The lobby is razzle-dazzle LED, marble and riveted steel, but the game room looks like a start-up HQ.

23 PIANOFIGHT
www.pianofight.com

Watch San Francisco make merciless fun of itself at PianoFight supperclub, featuring an unruly line-up of lectures with drunken experts at WasTED Talks, smartphone-hacker murder mysteries and midnight Friday comedy showcases.

24 OASIS
www.sfoasis.com

Forget what you've learned about drag on TV – at this dedicated dragstravaganza venue, drag is so fearless, freaky and funny, you'll laugh until it stops hurting.

25 BOURBON AND BRANCH
www.bourbonandbranch.com

'Don't even think of asking for a cosmo', read House Rules at this Prohibition-era speakeasy, recognisable by its deliciously misleading Anti-Saloon League sign. For award-winning cocktails in the liquored-up library, whisper the password ('books').

26 SIGHTGLASS COFFEE
www.sightglasscoffee.com

Follow cult coffee aromas into this sunny SoMa warehouse, where family-grown, high-end bourbon-shrub coffee is roasted daily. Aficionados sip signature Owl's Howl Espresso downstairs, or head directly to the mezzanine Affogato Bar.

27 TERROIR NATURAL WINE MERCHANT

Whether red or white, your wine is green here – this wine bar specialises in natural-process, organic and biodynamic wines, with impressive lists from French and Italian producers.

28 FARM:TABLE
www.farmtablesf.com

A ray of sunshine in the concrete heart of the city, this plucky little cafe showcases seasonal California organics in just-baked breakfasts and farmstead-fresh lunches.

29 FERRY PLAZA FARMERS MARKET
www.cuesa.org

The pride and joy of SF foodies, the Ferry Building market showcases 50 to 100 prime purveyors of California-grown, organic produce, pasture-raised meats and gourmet-prepared foods at accessible prices.

30 BENU
www.benusf.com

SF has pioneered Asian fusion cuisine for 150 years, but the pan-Pacific innovation chef-owner Corey Lee brings to the plate in this restaurant is gasp-inducing. Try the *foie-gras* soup dumplings.

VANCOUVER

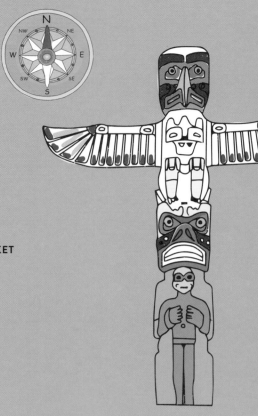

Feast your eyes (and your belly) on the culinary, cultural and outdoor delights this modern city has to offer.

1. CARNEGIE CENTRE
2. VOGUE THEATRE
3. BIERCRAFT BISTRO
4. PEKOE TEA LOUNGE
5. VIRTUOUS PIE
6. CORKSCREW INN
7. VANCOUVER AQUARIUM
8. GRAVITY POPE
9. A-MAZE-ING LAUGHTER
10. PACIFIC SPIRIT REGIONAL PARK
11. SECOND BEACH
12. JERICHO BEACH
13. SEABUS
14. MUSEUM OF VANCOUVER
15. KITSILANO FARMERS MARKET
16. THE WOLF & HOUND
17. STANLEY PARK
18. MUSEUM OF ANTHROPOLOGY
19. VANCOUVER ART GALLERY
20. GRANVILLE ISLAND PUBLIC MARKET
21. BLOEDEL CONSERVATORY
22. GROUSE MOUNTAIN
23. ST REGIS HOTEL
24. ROSEWOOD HOTEL GEORGIA
25. WEST
26. FORAGE
27. PUREBREAD
28. GALLERY OF BC CERAMICS
29. MINTAGE
30. REGIONAL ASSEMBLY OF TEXT

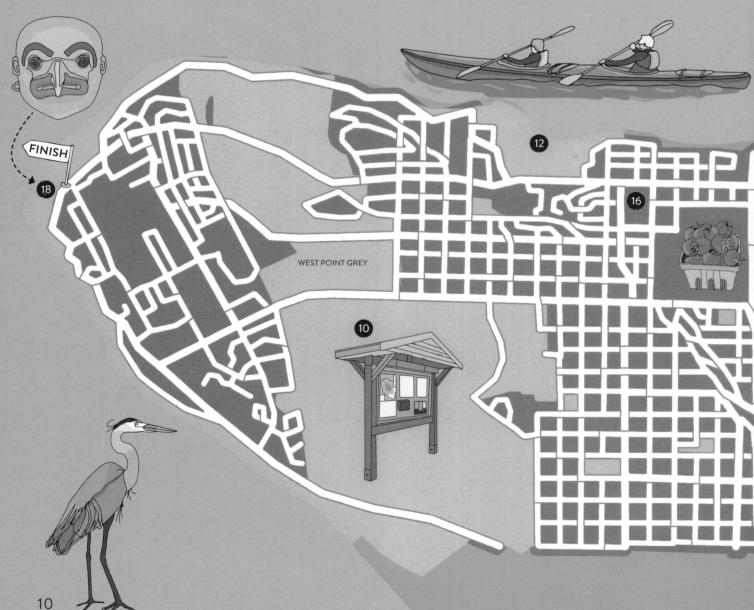

FINISH

18

12

16

WEST POINT GREY

10

WEST END

KITSILANO

JTUS RIDGE

STRATHCONA

MOUNT
PLEASANT

START

11

VANCOUVER

Walkable neighbourhoods, drink-and-dine delights and memorable cultural and outdoor activities framed by dramatic vistas – there's a glassful of reasons to love this lotusland metropolis. Whether discovering coffee shops, hipster haunts, indie bars or heritage-house beachfronts and browsable stores, you'll find this city perfect for easy-access urban exploration. And the outdoors is never far away; Vancouverites really can ski in the morning and hit the beach in the afternoon.

① CARNEGIE CENTRE

The city's first public library was a landmark corner building funded by US philanthropist Andrew Carnegie. Now a community centre for services provided to residents of the Downtown Eastside, it's still a handsome edifice to glance at on your way through the area.

② VOGUE THEATRE

www.voguetheatre.com

A 1940s heritage venue – check out the retro neon figure perched on the top of the streamlined exterior – the Vogue was bought and refurbished a few years back. Happily, the refurb didn't change much and this is a great old-school venue to see bands.

③ BIERCRAFT BISTRO

With a chatty, wood-lined interior plus two popular street-side patios, this beer-forward resto-bar is a great spot for ale aficionados. Dive into the astonishing array of Belgian tipples and compare them to some choice microbrews from British Columbia and the US.

④ PEKOE TEA LOUNGE

A restorative respite from busy Broadway, this locals' favourite is ideal for visiting tea nuts. Choose from dozens of varieties from around the world (nutcracker oolong recommended), then sink into a coveted sofa seat at the back of the store.

⑤ VIRTUOUS PIE

Named for the fact that its pizzas are entirely 'plant-based', this inviting vegan pizzeria, with its communal tables and mood lighting, has the look of a cool lounge bar. Arrive off-peak to sidestep the rush and dive into a menu of intriguing one-person pies with inventive fusion-esque toppings.

⑥ CORKSCREW INN

www.corkscrewinn.com

This immaculate, gable-roofed hotel appears to have a drinking problem: it houses a little museum, available only to guests, that's lined with quirky corkscrews and antique vineyard tools.

⑦ VANCOUVER AQUARIUM

www.vanaqua.org

Stanley Park's biggest draw, the aquarium is home to 9000 water-loving critters – including sharks, wolf eels and a somewhat shy octopus. There's also a small walk-through rainforest area of birds, turtles and a statue-still sloth.

⑧ GRAVITY POPE

This unisex temple of footwear is a dangerous place to come if you have a shoe fetish – best not to bring more than one credit card. Quality and designer *élan* are the keys here and you can expect to slip into Vancouver's best selection of fashion-forward clogs, wedges, mules and classy runners.

⑨ A-MAZE-ING LAUGHTER

Vancouver's most-photographed public artwork is just a few steps from English Bay Beach. Expect to see groups of smiling visitors snapping shots of the 14 oversized bronzes, each of them looking like they're about to explode with overabundant giggles.

⑩ PACIFIC SPIRIT REGIONAL PARK

www.pacificspiritparksociety.org

This stunning 763-hectare park stretches from Burrard Inlet to the North Arm of the Fraser River, a smashing spot to explore with 70km (43.5 miles) of walking, jogging and cycling trails; a bird and plant haven.

⑪ SECOND BEACH

Second Beach is a family-friendly area on Stanley Park's western side, with a grassy playground, an ice-cream-serving concession and the Stanley Park Pitch & Putt course. Its main attraction is the seasonal outdoor swimming pool.

⑫ JERICHO BEACH

An activity-lover's idyll, Jericho is great if you just want to putter along the beach, clamber over driftwood and catch stunning views of downtown. It's popular with locals on summer evenings, so expect impromptu but civilised beach gatherings, where discreet coolers of beer may appear.

⑬ SEABUS

The iconic SeaBus shuttle is part of the TransLink transit system and it operates throughout the day, taking 12 minutes to cross Burrard Inlet between Waterfront Station and Lonsdale Quay in North Vancouver.

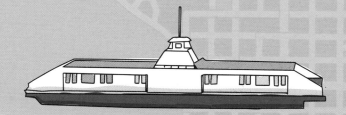

14 MUSEUM OF VANCOUVER

The MOV houses cool temporary exhibitions and hosts evening events for culturally minded adults. There are superbly evocative displays on local 1950s pop culture and 1960s hippie counterculture, plus a shimmering gallery of vintage neon signs from around the city.

15 KITSILANO FARMERS MARKET

Kitsilano's best excuse to get out and hang with the locals, this seasonal farmers market is one of the city's most popular. Arrive early and you'll have the pick of freshly plucked local fruit and veg, such as sweet strawberries and flavourful heirloom tomatoes.

16 THE WOLF & HOUND

The nearest good pub to UBC and one of Vancouver's best Irish watering holes; you'll find plenty of students avoiding their assignments here. They come to watch sports in the denlike back room or to catch free live music, often of the Celtic persuasion, on most weekends.

17 STANLEY PARK

This magnificent 404-hectare park combines excellent attractions with a mystical natural aura. Don't miss a stroll or cycle around the 8.8 km (5.5 miles) seawall and past the park's popular totem poles.

18 MUSEUM OF ANTHROPOLOGY
www.moa.ubc.ca

Vancouver's best museum is studded with spectacular First Nations totem poles and breathtaking carvings – but it's also teeming with artefacts from cultures around the world, from Polynesian instruments to Cantonese opera costumes.

19 VANCOUVER ART GALLERY
www.vanartgallery.bc.ca

A vital part of the city's cultural scene, the VAG hosts contemporary exhibitions – often showcasing Vancouver's renowned photoconceptualists – combined with blockbuster international travelling shows.

20 GRANVILLE ISLAND PUBLIC MARKET
www.granvilleisland.com/public-market

Granville Island's highlight is the covered Public Market, a multisensory smorgasbord of fish, cheese, fruit and bakery treats. From June to September, there's also an alfresco farmers market.

21 BLOEDEL CONSERVATORY
www.vandusengarden.org

This balmy, triodetic-domed conservatory is an ideal rainy-day warm-up spot, as well as Vancouver's best-value attraction: for little more than the price of a latte, you'll find tropical plants bristling with bright-plumaged birds.

22 GROUSE MOUNTAIN
www.grousemountain.com

This mountain-top playground offers smashing views of downtown glittering in the water below. In summer, Skyride gondola tickets include access to lumberjack shows, alpine hiking, bird-of-prey displays and a grizzly bear refuge.

23 ST REGIS HOTEL
www.stregishotel.com

An art-lined boutique sleepover in a 1913 heritage shell. Befitting its age, almost all the rooms seem to be a different size, with leather-look wallpaper, earth-toned bedspreads, flatscreen TVs and multimedia hubs.

24 ROSEWOOD HOTEL GEORGIA
www.rosewoodhotels.com

Vancouver's current 'It' hotel underwent a spectacular renovation a few years back that brought the 1927-built landmark back to its golden-age glory. The hotel's rooms take a classic, elegant approach.

25 WEST
www.westrestaurant.com

This sleek, but never snobbish, fine-dining restaurant is committed to superb West Coast meals with ultra-attentive service and a great wine selection. Ideal for a classy night out.

26 FORAGE
www.foragevancouver.com

A champion of the local farm-to-table scene, this sustainability-friendly restaurant is the perfect way to sample the flavours of the region. Brunch has become a firm local favourite.

27 PUREBREAD
www.purebread.ca

When Whistler's favourite bakery opened here, salivating Vancouverites began flocking en masse. Expect to stand slack-jawed as you try to choose from a cornucopia of cakes, pastries and bars.

28 GALLERY OF BC CERAMICS
www.bcpotters.com

The star of Granville Island's arts-and-crafts shops and the public face of the Potters Guild of BC, this excellent spot exhibits and sells the striking works of its member artists.

29 MINTAGE
www.mintagevintage.com

This is where Drive hipsters add a little vintage glam to their look and there's a Western-saloon feel to the interior, but don't be fooled – this is one of the city's most kaleidoscopically eclectic stores.

30 REGIONAL ASSEMBLY OF TEXT
www.assemblyoftext.com

This stationery and gift store is an ironic antidote to the digital age, luring ink-stained locals with its journals, handmade pencil boxes and T-shirts printed with typewriter motifs. Check out the tiny under-the-stairs gallery showcasing worldwide zines.

NEW YORK

Be careful you don't trip on your journey, as you'll be looking skyward in awe. Follow the grid system of streets and avenues to reach your destination.

UPPER EAST SIDE

HARLEM

APOLLO
THE APOLLO THE
WHO CAP ARE

19

10

7

17

22

UPPER WEST SIDE

30

6

16

25

MoMA

2

HELL'S KITCHEN

18

1. CHRYSLER BUILDING
2. EMPIRE STATE BUILDING
3. GRAND CENTRAL TERMINAL
4. TIMES SQUARE
5. ROCKEFELLER CENTER
6. MUSEUM OF MODERN ART
7. CENTRAL PARK
8. BROOKLYN BRIDGE
9. NATIONAL SEPTEMBER 11 MEMORIAL
10. APOLLO THEATER
11. LOWER EAST SIDE TENEMENT MUSEUM
12. GILD HALL
13. CHELSEA MARKET
14. MUSEUM OF JEWISH HERITAGE
15. HIGH LINE
16. AMERICAN MUSEUM OF NATURAL HISTORY
17. METROPOLITAN MUSEUM OF ART
18. YOTEL
19. HARLEM FLOPHOUSE
20. GREENWICH HOTEL
21. KNICKERBOCKER
22. FRICK COLLECTION
23. DOUGH
24. MOMOFUKU NOODLE BAR
25. LE BERNARDIN
26. ABC CARPET & HOME
27. OPENING CEREMONY
28. PHILIP WILLIAMS POSTERS
29. STRAND BOOK STORE
30. BERGDORF GOODMAN

START

EAST VILLAGE

GREENWICH VILLAGE

TWO BRIDGES

LOWER MANHATTAN

FINISH

NEW YORK

Epicentre of the arts. Dining and shopping capital. Trendsetter. New York City wears many crowns, and spreads an irresistible feast for all. When the sun sinks slowly beyond the Hudson and luminous skyscrapers light up the night, New York transforms into one grand stage. There's never been a better time to dine in New York: the city has become a hotbed of seasonal and locally sourced cuisine, from coffee roasting and whiskey distilling to chocolate- and cheese-making.

① CHRYSLER BUILDING

Designed by William Van Alen in 1930, the 77-floor Chrysler Building is prime-time architecture: a fusion of Modern and Gothic aesthetics, adorned with steel eagles and a spire that screams Bride of Frankenstein.

② EMPIRE STATE BUILDING
www.esbnyc.com

This limestone classic was built in just 410 days – using seven million hours of labour during the Great Depression – and the views from its 86th-floor outdoor deck and 102nd-floor indoor deck are heavenly.

③ GRAND CENTRAL TERMINAL
www.grandcentralterminal.com

Completed in 1913, Grand Central Terminal – more commonly, if technically incorrectly, called Grand Central Station – is one of New York's beaux-arts beauties, adorned with Tennessee-marble floors and Italian-marble ticket counters.

④ TIMES SQUARE
www.timessquarenyc.org

Love it or hate it, the intersection of Broadway and Seventh Ave (aka: Times Square) pumps out the NYC of the global imagination – yellow cabs, golden arches, soaring skyscrapers and razzle-dazzle Broadway marquees.

⑤ ROCKEFELLER CENTER
www.rockefellercenter.com

This 22-acre 'city within a city' debuted in the Great Depression, with developer John D Rockefeller Jr footing the $100 million price tag. It was America's first multi-use retail, entertainment and office space.

⑥ MUSEUM OF MODERN ART
www.moma.org

Modern-art scene superstar, MoMA's galleries scintillate with heavyweights: Van Gogh, Matisse, Picasso, Warhol, Lichtenstein, Rothko, Pollock and Bourgeois. The permanent collection has four levels, with prints, books and the unmissable Contemporary Galleries.

⑦ CENTRAL PARK
www.centralparknyc.org

One of the world's most renowned green spaces, Central Park spreads across 843 acres of rolling meadows, boulder-studded outcroppings, elm-lined walkways, manicured European-style gardens, a lake and a reservoir.

⑧ BROOKLYN BRIDGE

Connecting Brooklyn and Manhattan, Brooklyn Bridge was the world's first steel suspension bridge. Indeed, when it opened in 1883, its 1596ft span was the longest in history.

⑨ NATIONAL SEPTEMBER 11 MEMORIAL
www.911memorial.org

The focal point of the National September 11 Memorial is Reflecting Absence, two imposing reflecting pools that occupy the very footprints of the ill-fated twin towers.

⑩ APOLLO THEATER
www.apollotheater.org

The Apollo is an intrinsic part of Harlem history and culture. A leading space for concerts and rallies since 1914, its stage hosted virtually every major black artist in the 1930s and '40s.

⑪ LOWER EAST SIDE TENEMENT MUSEUM
www.tenement.org

This museum puts the neighbourhood's heartbreaking but inspiring heritage on full display in three recreated turn-of-the-20th-century tenement apartments. Visits are available only as part of guided tours.

⑫ GILD HALL
www.thompsonhotels.com/hotels/gild-hall

Boutique and brilliant, hotel Gild Hall's entryway leads to a bi-level library and wine bar that exudes hunting-lodge chic. Rooms fuse Euro elegance and American comfort, with kingsize beds in minimalist surroundings.

13 CHELSEA MARKET
www.chelseamarket.com

In a shining example of redevelopment and preservation, the Chelsea Market has transformed a former factory into a shopping concourse that caters to foodies. More than two dozen food vendors ply their temptations.

14 MUSEUM OF JEWISH HERITAGE
www.mjhnyc.org

An evocative waterfront museum exploring all aspects of modern Jewish identity and culture, from religious traditions to artistic accomplishments. The core exhibition includes a detailed exploration of the Holocaust.

15 HIGH LINE
www.thehighline.org

This eye-catching attraction is one of New York's best-loved green spaces, drawing visitors who come to stroll, sit and picnic 30ft above the city, enjoying fabulous views of Manhattan's ever-changing urban landscape.

16 AMERICAN MUSEUM OF NATURAL HISTORY
www.amnh.org

Founded in 1869, this classic museum contains a veritable wonderland of more than 30 million artefacts – like menacing dinosaur skeletons – as well as the cutting-edge planetarium of the Rose Center for Earth & Space.

17 METROPOLITAN MUSEUM OF ART
www.metmuseum.org

This encyclopedic museum, founded in 1870, houses one of the world's largest art collections. Known colloquially as 'The Met', it attracts over six million visitors a year to its 17 acres of galleries.

18 YOTEL
www.yotel.com

Part futuristic spaceport, part Austin Powers set, this uber-cool 669-room hotel bases its rooms on airplane classes: Premium Cabin (Economy), First Cabins (Business) and VIP Suites (First).

19 HARLEM FLOPHOUSE
www.harlemflophouse.com

Rekindle Harlem's Jazz Age in this 1890s townhouse hotel, its nostalgic rooms decked out in brass beds, polished wood floors and vintage radios (set to a local jazz station).

20 GREENWICH HOTEL
www.thegreenwichhotel.com

From the plush drawing room (complete with crackling fire) to the lantern-lit pool inside a reconstructed Japanese farmhouse, nothing about Robert De Niro's Greenwich Hotel is generic.

21 KNICKERBOCKER
theknickerbocker.com

The 330-room Knickerbocker hotel is back in business after a luxurious, $240-million refurbishment and exudes a restrained, monochromatic elegance. Rooms are dashingly chic, hushed and modern.

22 FRICK COLLECTION
www.frick.org

This spectacular art collection sits in a mansion built by prickly steel magnate Henry Clay Frick, with more than a dozen splendid rooms displaying masterpieces by Titian, Vermeer, Gilbert Stuart, El Greco and Goya.

23 DOUGH
www.doughdoughnuts.com

This tiny, out-of-the-way spot is a bit of a trek, but worth it if you're a pastry fan. Puffy raised doughnuts are dipped in a changing array of glazes: divinity for the tongue.

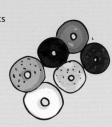

24 MOMOFUKU NOODLE BAR
noodlebar-ny.momofuku.com

With just 30 stools and a no-reservations policy, you'll always have to wait to cram into this bustling phenomenon. Queue up for the namesake special: homemade ramen noodles in broth.

25 LE BERNARDIN
www.le-bernardin.com

Triple-Michelin-starred Le Bernardin remains a luxe, fine-dining holy grail. At the helm is French-born celebrity chef Éric Ripert, whose deceptively simple-looking seafood often borders on the transcendental.

26 ABC CARPET & HOME
www.abchome.com

A mecca for home designers and decorators brainstorming ideas, this beautifully curated, seven-level store is a temple to good taste and heaves with all sorts of furnishings, small and large.

27 OPENING CEREMONY
www.openingceremony.us

Unisex store Opening Ceremony is famed for its never-boring edit of A-list indie labels. The place showcases a changing, international roster of names; complementing them is Opening Ceremony's own avant-garde creations.

28 PHILIP WILLIAMS POSTERS
www.postermuseum.com

You'll find nearly half a million posters in this cavernous treasure trove of a retail gallery, from oversized French advertisements for perfume and cognac to Soviet film posters and retro-fab promos for TWA.

29 STRAND BOOK STORE
www.strandbooks.com

Beloved and legendary, the iconic Strand embodies downtown NYC's intellectual bona fides – a bibliophile's Oz, where generations of book lovers carrying the store's trademark tote bags happily lose themselves for hours.

30 BERGDORF GOODMAN
www.bergdorfgoodman.com

Not merely loved for its Christmas windows (the city's best), plush store BG, at this location since 1928, leads the fashion race, led by its industry-leading fashion director Linda Fargo.

BUENOS AIRES

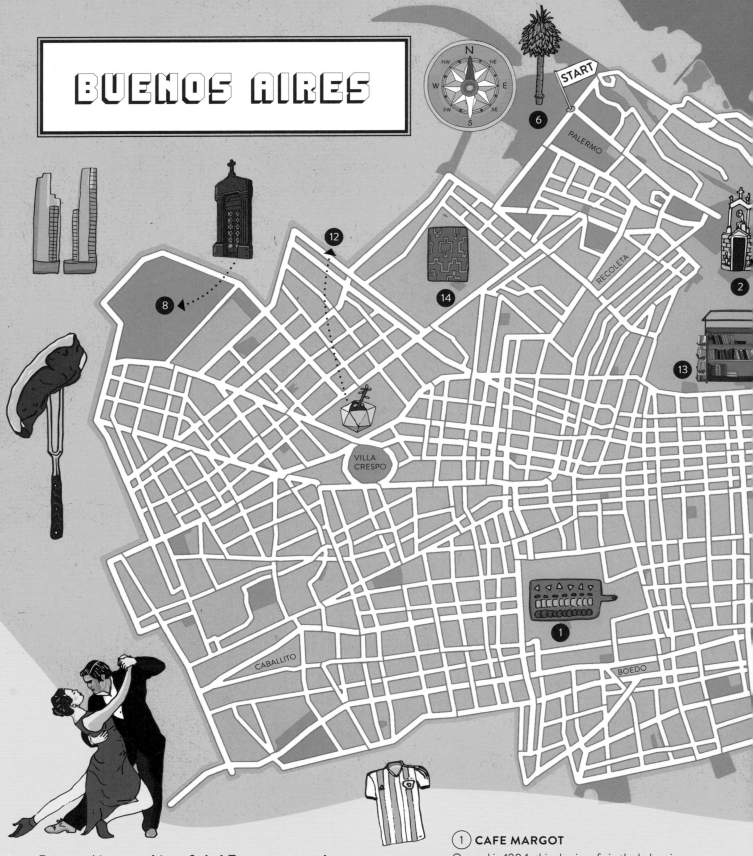

START

6

PALERMO

RECOLETA

12

8

14

2

13

VILLA
CRESPO

1

CABALLITO

BOEDO

Buenos Aires combines faded European grandeur with Latin passion. Sexy and alive, this beautiful city gets under your skin. The food scene is increasingly dynamic, but for many travellers it's the city's carnivorous pleasures that shine. The tango is possibly Buenos Aires' greatest contribution to the outside world, a steamy strut that's been described as 'making love in the vertical position'.

1 CAFE MARGOT

Opened in 1904, this classic cafe in the bohemian neighbourhood of Boedo is a typically *porteño* spot to relax with a *picada* (a platter of cold cuts, cheese and olives) and a bottle of wine.

2 CEMENTERIO DE LA RECOLETA

www.cementeriorecoleta.com

This cemetery is a top attraction. You can wander for hours in this incredible city of the dead, where the 'streets' are lined with statues and marble mausoleums.

③ MANZANA DE LAS LUCES
www.manazadelasluces.org

In colonial times, historic landmark Manzana de las Luces was Buenos Aires' most important centre of culture and learning, and today the block still symbolises education and enlightenment.

④ CENTRO CULTURAL KIRCHNER
www.culturalkirchner.gob.ar

Now a breathtaking cultural centre, but formerly the central post office, this vast beaux-arts structure – that takes up an entire city block – holds art galleries, events and auditoriums.

⑦ EL CAMINITO
La Boca's most famous street and 'open air' museum is a magnet for visitors, who come to see its brightly painted houses and snap photographs of the painted figures and tango dancers.

⑧ CEMENTERIO DE LA CHACARITA
This large cemetery is much less visited by tourists than Recoleta, but its most elaborate tombs are no less impressive.

⑨ IMAGINE HOTEL
www.imaginehotelboutique.com

This beautiful guesthouse in a traditional *chorizo*-style house (a long, narrow sausage-like building) offers nine appealing rooms, all individually decorated with rustic, yet upscale, furniture.

⑩ IL MATTERELLO
This Genovese trattoria serves up some of the best pasta in town, including al dente *tagliatelle alla rúcola* (tagliatelle with arugula), and tiramisu for dessert.

⑪ EL REFUERZO BAR ALMACÉN
www.facebook.com/elrefuerzobaralmacen

The dining room fills up quickly at this small *almacén*-(warehouse) style restaurant. There's an excellent wine list to match the menu of top-notch dishes written on blackboards on the walls.

⑫ BOSQUE
www.bosque2.mitiendanube.com

A charming range of arts and crafts with a botanical bent is sold in this tiny boutique. The woodland theme is evident in illustrations, plates, ceramics and cushions.

⑬ EL ATENEO GRAND SPLENDID
www.yenny-elateneo.com/local/grand-splendid

This glorious bookstore (2000) in a converted theatre (1919) continues to flourish in the age of the Kindle. The original features have been preserved, including the beautiful painted cupola and balconies.

⑭ ELEMENTOS ARGENTINOS
www.elementosargentinos.com.ar

The high-quality carpets, rugs and blankets sold here are hand-dyed, hand-woven on a loom and fair trade; the owners work with cooperatives and NGOs to help the communities in northwestern Argentina.

⑤ FERIA DE SAN TELMO
www.feriadesantelmo.com

On Sundays, San Telmo's main drag becomes a sea of both locals and tourists browsing craft stalls, waiting at vendors' carts, poking through glass ornaments and listening to street performances.

⑥ PARQUE 3 DE FEBRERO
This sweeping parkland abounds with small lakes and gazebos. There's also a monument to literary greats called El Jardín de los Poetas (Garden of Poets).

⑮ PLAZA DE MAYO

Surrounded by the Casa Rosada, the Cabildo and the city's main cathedral, Plaza de Mayo is the place where Argentines gather in protest or celebration. At the centre is the Pirámide de Mayo, a white obelisk built to mark the first anniversary of independence from Spain.

RIO

Feel the samba beat and prepare to be seduced by carnival-spirited Rio de Janeiro – make sure you find your way, as well as your rhythm!

START

GÁVEA

LEBLON

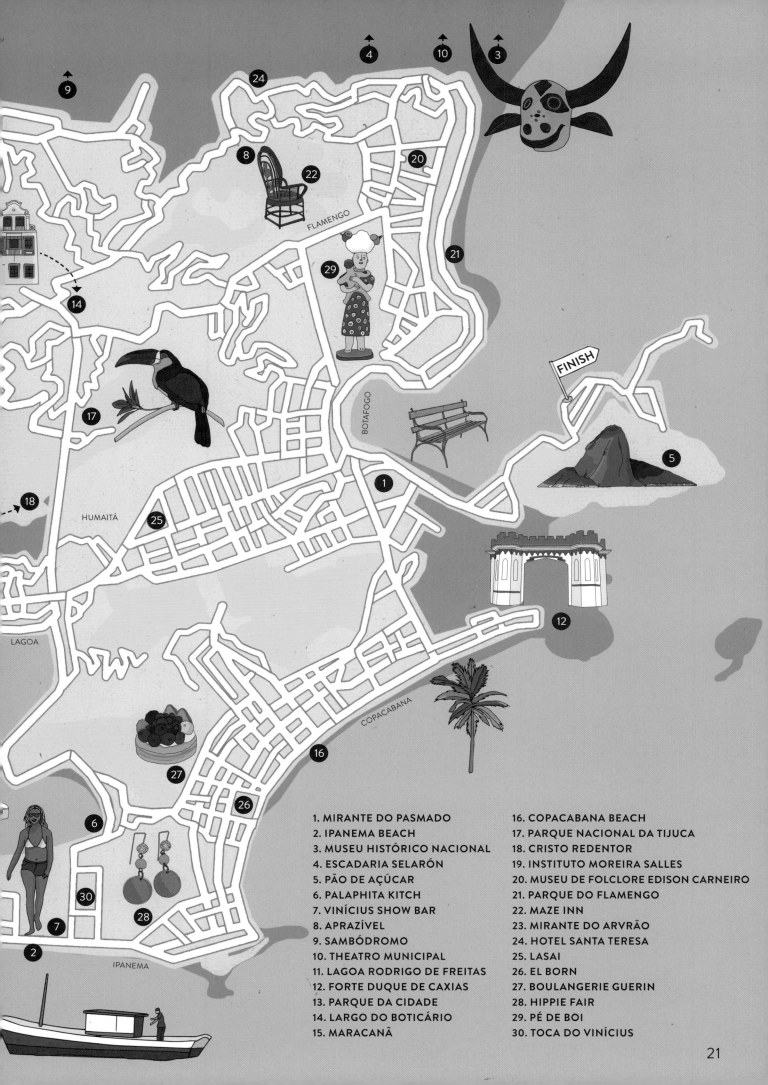

FLAMENGO

BOTAFOGO

FINISH

HUMAITÁ

LAGOA

COPACABANA

IPANEMA

1. MIRANTE DO PASMADO
2. IPANEMA BEACH
3. MUSEU HISTÓRICO NACIONAL
4. ESCADARIA SELARÓN
5. PÃO DE AÇÚCAR
6. PALAPHITA KITCH
7. VINÍCIUS SHOW BAR
8. APRAZÍVEL
9. SAMBÓDROMO
10. THEATRO MUNICIPAL
11. LAGOA RODRIGO DE FREITAS
12. FORTE DUQUE DE CAXIAS
13. PARQUE DA CIDADE
14. LARGO DO BOTICÁRIO
15. MARACANÃ

16. COPACABANA BEACH
17. PARQUE NACIONAL DA TIJUCA
18. CRISTO REDENTOR
19. INSTITUTO MOREIRA SALLES
20. MUSEU DE FOLCLORE EDISON CARNEIRO
21. PARQUE DO FLAMENGO
22. MAZE INN
23. MIRANTE DO ARVRÃO
24. HOTEL SANTA TERESA
25. LASAI
26. EL BORN
27. BOULANGERIE GUERIN
28. HIPPIE FAIR
29. PÉ DE BOI
30. TOCA DO VINÍCIUS

21

RIO

From Ipanema to Copacabana, Rio's beaches have long seduced visitors. The city is also fringed by lushly forested mountains and a string of tiny islands, with a pool of activities available from sailing to hang gliding. But above all, Rio knows how to party. *Carnaval*, and the build up to it, is the most obvious manifestation of this celebratory spirit. Music is the lifeblood of this city; the samba being synonymous with Rio, which you can hear all over town.

1 MIRANTE DO PASMADO

Sweeping views of Enseada de Botafogo, Pão de Açúcar and Corcovado await visitors who make the journey up Pasmado. The viewpoint is best reached in early morning or late afternoon, when the light is at its best for capturing the postcard panorama.

2 IPANEMA BEACH

You've seen the photos and heard the jazzy song ('Girl from Ipanema'), but nothing quite compares to kicking off your Havaianas and strolling along the sun-drenched golden sands of Rio's most famous beach.

3 MUSEU HISTÓRICO NACIONAL

www.museuhistoriconacional.com.br

Housed in the colonial arsenal, which dates from 1764, this impressive museum contains relics relating to the history of Brazil from its founding to its early days as a republic.

4 ESCADARIA SELARÓN

The steps leading up from Rua Joaquim Silva became a work of art when Chilean-born artist Jorge Selarón decided to cover them with colourful mosaics, all dedicated to the Brazilian people.

5 PÃO DE AÇÚCAR

One of Rio's dazzling icons, Pão de Açúcar (Sugarloaf Mountain) offers a vision of Rio at its most disarming. There are many good times to make the ascent, but sunset on a clear day is the most rewarding.

6 PALAPHITA KITCH

www.palaphitakitch.com.br

This open-air, thatched-roof lounge and restaurant with rustic bamboo furniture and flickering tiki torches is a peaceful setting on the edge of the lake and a great spot for a sundowner. It's a popular spot with couples.

7 VINÍCIUS SHOW BAR

Billing itself as the 'temple of bossa nova', this intimate space makes a fine setting to listen to first-rate bossa nova, and occasional Música Popular Brasileira (MPB) and samba.

8 APRAZÍVEL

www.aprazivel.com.br

Hidden high up in Santa Teresa, this restaurant offers beautiful views and a lush garden setting. Grilled fish and roasted dishes showcase the country's culinary highlights of land and sea.

9 SAMBÓDROMO

www.sambadrome.com

The epicentre of Rio's Carnaval, the Oscar Niemeyer-designed Sambódromo venue was completed in 1984. During the big parades, come for fantastic views from the stands across elaborate floats, whirling dancers and pounding drums.

10 THEATRO MUNICIPAL

www.theatromunicipal.rj.gov.br

This gorgeous art nouveau theatre provides the setting for Rio's best opera, ballet and symphonic concerts. The theatre seats 2400, and sight lines are generally good.

11 LAGOA RODRIGO DE FREITAS

One of the city's most picturesque spots, this lake is encircled by a 7.2km (4.5 mile) walking and cycling path. Bikes and paddle boats are available for hire from stands along the east side.

12 FORTE DUQUE DE CAXIAS

More commonly known as Forte do Leme, this military base is open to the public. Visitors can walk to the top of Morro do Leme (Leme Mountain) along a steep 800m trail that passes through Atlantic rainforest.

13 PARQUE DA CIDADE

www.rio.rj.gov.br/cultura

On the outer reaches of Gávea, this lush park of native Mata Atlantica rainforest and replanted secondary forest provides a refreshing escape from the heavy traffic on nearby Rua Marques de São Vicente.

⑭ LARGO DO BOTICÁRIO

The brightly painted, but sadly dilapidated, houses on this picturesque plaza date from the early 19th century. Largo do Boticário was named in honour of the Portuguese gentleman who once ran a *boticário* (pharmacy) used by the royal family.

⑮ MARACANÃ

www.suderj.rj.gov.br/maracana.asp

For a quasi-psychedelic experience, go to a *futebol* match at Maracanã, Brazil's temple to football. Matches here rate amongst the most exciting in the world.

⑯ COPACABANA BEACH

A magnificent confluence of land and sea, the long, scalloped beach of Copacabana extends for some 4km (2.5 miles), with a flurry of activity by football players, cariocas, tourists, favela kids and beach vendors.

⑰ PARQUE NACIONAL DA TIJUCA

This 39 sq km (15 sq mile) tropical jungle preserve is an exuberant green, with beautiful trees, creeks and waterfalls, mountainous terrain and high peaks. It has an excellent, well-marked trail system.

⑱ CRISTO REDENTOR

www.corcovado.com.br

Standing atop Corcovado, Cristo Redentor gazes out over Rio, a placid expression on his well-crafted face. At night, the brightly lit open-armed statue is visible from nearly every part of the city.

⑲ INSTITUTO MOREIRA SALLES

www.ims.com.br

This beautiful cultural centre hosts impressive exhibitions showcasing the works of some of Brazil's best photographers and artists, amid gardens complete with an artificial lake and a flowing river.

⑳ MUSEU DE FOLCLORE EDISON CARNEIRO

www.cnfcp.gov.br

This museum is an excellent introduction to Brazilian folk art, particularly that from the northeast, and comprises 1400 pieces like Candomblé costumes, ceramic figurines and religious costumes used in festivals.

㉑ PARQUE DO FLAMENGO

Parque do Flamengo was the result of a landfill project that levelled the São Antônio hill in 1965. The 1.2 sq km (1.5 sq mile) of land reclaimed from the sea now stages every manner of carioca outdoor activity.

㉒ MAZE INN

www.jazzrio.com

Set in Tavares Bastos favela, the Maze Inn is a fantastic place to overnight for those looking for an alternative view of Rio. The guesthouse's veranda offers stunning views of the bay and Pão de Açúcar.

㉓ MIRANTE DO ARVRÃO

mirantedoarvrao.com.br

A surprising find in Vidigal, the Mirante do Arvrão hotel has beautifully set rooms, the best of which offer gorgeous views over the ocean. It's worth paying extra for a deluxe room.

㉔ HOTEL SANTA TERESA

www.santateresahotelrio.com

What is probably the finest boutique hotel in Rio is set in a lavishly restored building that was part of a coffee plantation in the 19th century.

㉕ LASAI

www.lasai.com.br

Inside an elegant early 20th-century house in Humaitá, restaurant Lasai has dazzled critics and foodies with its deliciously inventive cuisine. Chef Rafa Costa e Silva puts his skills to brilliant use.

㉖ EL BORN

Named after Barcelona's hippest, foodie-loving neighbourhood, restaurant El Born fires up some of Rio's best tapas plates: think Galician-style octopus, spicy prawns and tender Iberian ham.

㉗ BOULANGERIE GUERIN

Serving Rio's best croissants, pains au chocolat and eclairs, this French patisserie was an instant success upon opening in 2012. Prices are high, but so is the quality.

㉘ HIPPIE FAIR

The Zona Sul's most famous market, the Hippie Fair (aka Feira de Arte de Ipanema) has artwork, jewellery, handicrafts, clothing and souvenirs for sale. Stalls in the plaza's four corners sell tasty food.

㉙ PÉ DE BOI

www.pedeboi.com.br

Pé de Boi feels more like an art gallery than a handicrafts shop, owing to the high quality of the wood and ceramic works, and the tapestries, sculptures and weavings.

㉚ TOCA DO VINÍCIUS

www.tocadovinicius.com.br

Bossa nova fans shouldn't miss this store. In addition to its ample CD and vinyl selection of contemporary and old performers, it also sells music scores and composition books.

LISBON

Seven cinematic hillsides overlooking the Rio Tejo cradle Lisbon's postcard-perfect panorama of cobbled alleyways, ancient ruins and white-domed cathedrals – a captivating recipe crafted over centuries. Lisbon's strategic seaside position on Europe's doorstep means a bounty of fresh seafood rules the city's kitchens. And when it comes to the evening, student dives, traditional fado houses and upscale wine bars merrily coexist in amongst the winding streets.

START

PRÍNCIPE REAL

BAIRRO ALTO

LAPA

11

7

SANTOS-O-VELHO

PRAZERES

6

4

② MANTEIGARIA

Baking *pastéis de nata* really is rocket science in Lisbon. But this born-again butter factory gets it just right – crisp tarts that flake just so are filled with luscious cream and served with good strong coffee and smiles at this bright modern cafe.

① ASCENSOR DA BICA

www.transporteslisboa.pt

This funicular has been creaking arthritically up the steep, narrow Rua da Bica de Duarte Belo since 1892. Jump aboard to save your legs and enjoy fleeting glimpses of the Rio Tejo and pastel-hued houses.

③ MIRADOURO DA SENHORA DO MONTE

Lisbon spreads out before you at Graça's highest of the high, Miradouro da Senhora do Monte. Come for the relaxed vibe and the best views of the castle on the hill opposite. It's a short walk west (along Rua da Senhora do Monte) of the tram 28 stop on Rua da Graça.

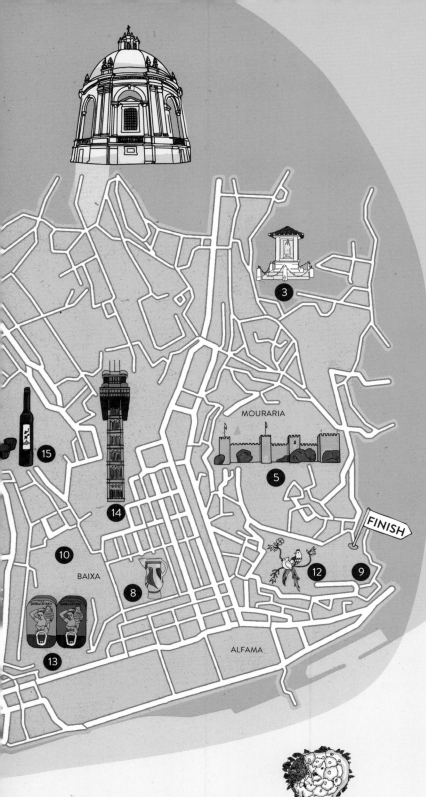

6 MUSEU NACIONAL DE ARTE ANTIGA
www.museudearteantiga.pt

Set in a lemon-fronted, 17th-century palace, the Museu presents a star-studded collection of European and Asian paintings and decorative arts.

7 MUSEU DA MARIONETA
www.museudamarioneta.pt

Discover your inner child at this Geppetto's workshop housed in the 17th-century Convento das Bernardas. See Punch and his Portuguese equivalent Dom Roberto, plus international rarities.

8 NÚCLEO ARQUEOLÓGICO DA RUA DOS CORREEIROS
www.ind.millenniumbcp.pt

Hidden under the Millennium BCP bank building are layers of ruins dating from the Iron Age, discovered on a 1991 parking-lot dig.

9 MEMMO ALFAMA
www.memmoalfama.com

Slip down a narrow alley to reach these gorgeous boutique Alfama sleeps; a stunning conversion of a shoe-polish factory and former bakery.

10 ALMA
www.almalisboa.pt

A casual eatery with understated style plus Henrique Sá Pessoa's – one of Portugal's most talented chefs – outrageously good nouveau Portuguese cuisine.

11 EMBAIXADA
www.embaixadalx.pt

Take an exquisite 19th-century neo-Moorish palace and fill it with fashion, design and concept stores on the cutting-edge of cool and you have one of Lisbon's most exciting shopping experiences.

12 ARTE DA TERRA
www.aartedaterra.pt

In the stables of a centuries-old bishop's palace, Arte da Terra brims with authentic Portuguese crafts including Castello Branco embroideries, nativity figurines, hand-painted *azulejos* and *fado* CDs.

13 LOJA DAS CONSERVAS
www.facebook.com/lojadasconservas

A fascinating temple to tinned fish (or *conservas*), this shop is the result of an industry on its deathbed revived by savvy marketing.

14 SANTA JUSTA LIFT

Lisbon's only vertical street lift, built in 1902 and steam-powered until 1907, might seem uncannily familiar, because the neo-Gothic marvel is the handiwork of Raul Mésnier, Gustave Eiffel's apprentice.

15 GINGINHA DO CARMO
www.ginginhadocarmo.blogspot.pt

Tucked behind the Estação do Rossio, this newer *ginjinha* bar flaunts a slick, monochrome interior. It's a convivial spot for a *ginjinha* shot served in an edible chocolate cup.

4 MERCADO DA RIBEIRA
www.timeoutmarket.com

Doing trade in fresh fruit and veg, fish and flowers since 1892, this oriental-dome-topped market hall has been the word on everyone's lips since *Time Out* transformed half of it into a gourmet food court in 2014.

5 CASTELO DE SÃO JORGE
www.castelodesaojorge.pt

Towering dramatically above Lisbon, the mid-11th-century hilltop fortifications of Castelo de São Jorge sneak into almost every snapshot. Roam its snaking ramparts and pine-shaded courtyards for superlative views over the city.

DUBLIN

THE LIBERTIES

DAME DISTRICT

FINISH

A small capital with a huge reputation, Dublin's mix of heritage and hedonism will not disappoint. The city is a living museum of its history, with medieval castles and cathedrals alongside 18th-century architectural splendours. Dubliners are the greatest hosts of all, a charismatic bunch with soul, wit and sociability. The pub remains the alpha and omega of social interaction in Dublin and with more than 1000 of them spread about the city, you'll be spoilt for choice.

① **GUINNESS STOREHOUSE**
www.guinness-storehouse.com

The most popular visit in town is this multimedia homage to Guinness. The converted grain storehouse is a suitable cathedral in which to worship the black gold.

② **OLD LIBRARY & BOOK OF KELLS**
www.tcd.ie/library

Trinity's greatest treasures are found within the Old Library. The star of the show is the Book of Kells, a breathtaking, illuminated manuscript of the four Gospels of the New Testament.

START

DOCKLANDS

MERRION SQUARE

⑨

⑤ TEELING DISTILLERY
www.teelingwhiskey.com

The first new distillery in Dublin for 125 years, Teeling only began production in 2015 and it will be several years before any of the distillate can be called whisky.

⑥ JAMES JOYCE HOUSE OF THE DEAD

The young Joyce spent Christmases with his aunts in this house, which he later used as the setting for 'The Dead', the last story in *Dubliners*.

⑦ BUSWELL'S HOTEL
www.buswells.ie

This Dublin institution, open since 1882, has a long association with politicians, who wander across the road from Dáil Éireann to wet their beaks at the hotel bar.

⑧ DUBLIN COOKIE COMPANY
www.thedublincookieco.com

This neat little independent store's cookies are made fresh all day. As well as new and exciting flavours, it offers strong, aromatic coffee and chocolate or cookie-flavoured milk.

⑨ RESTAURANT PATRICK GUILBAUD
www.restaurantpatrickguilbaud.ie

Devotees of Ireland's only Michelin two-star proclaim Guillaume Lebrun's French haute cuisine the most exalted expression of the culinary arts.

⑩ TEMPLE BAR

The most photographed pub façade in Dublin, perhaps the world, the Temple Bar (aka Flannery's) is in the middle of the tourist precinct and is chock-a-block with visitors.

⑪ KEHOE'S

A favourite with all kinds of Dubliners, Kehoe's has a beautiful Victorian bar, a wonderful snug and plenty of other little nooks and crannies.

⑫ SMOCK ALLEY THEATRE
www.smockalley.com

This diverse theatre is hidden in a beautifully restored 17th-century building. Expect anything from opera to murder mystery nights, puppet shows and Shakespeare.

⑬ DEVITT'S
www.devittspub.ie

Pub Devitt's – aka the Cusack Stand – is one of the favourite places for the city's talented musicians to display their wares.

⑭ WHELAN'S
www.whelanslive.com

The singer-songwriter's spiritual home: when they're done pouring out the contents of their hearts on stage, you can find them filling up in the bar.

③ TRINITY COLLEGE
www.tcd.ie

Ireland's most prestigious university is a bucolic retreat in the heart of the city, recalling those far-off days when all good gentlemen came equipped with a passion for philosophy and a love of empire.

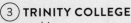

④ NATIONAL LEPRECHAUN MUSEUM
www.leprechaunmuseum.ie

Ostensibly designed as a child-friendly museum of Irish folklore, this is really a romper-room for kids sprinkled with bits of fairytale.

⑮ BARRY DOYLE DESIGN JEWELLERS
www.barrydoyledesign.com

Goldsmith Barry Doyle's upstairs shop sells exceptional handmade jewellery with Afro-Celtic influences.

LONDON

Join the hustle and bustle as you pass historic landmarks interspersed with striking modern architecture, and drink in the buzzing atmosphere and renowned culture as you go.

START

KENSINGTON

KNIGHTSBRIDGE

WESTMINSTER

SOHO

CHELSEA

HAMMERSMITH

VAUXHALL

SOU

CAMDEN LOCK

TWININGS
EST 1706

SHOREDITCH

HACKNEY

CITY OF LONDON

FINISH

1. ROYAL ALBERT HALL
2. IMPERIAL WAR MUSEUM
3. WHITECHAPEL GALLERY
4. VIKTOR WYND MUSEUM
5. ELFIN OAK
6. SPEAKERS' CORNER
7. BIG BEN
8. CHURCHILL WAR ROOMS
9. GEFFRYE MUSEUM
10. BOROUGH MARKET
11. LONDON EYE

12. TATE MODERN
13. LAMB & FLAG
14. SKY POD
15. CONNAUGHT BAR
16. RONNIE SCOTT'S
17. PRINCE CHARLES CINEMA
18. WIGMORE HALL
19. AMUSED MOOSE SOHO
20. JOHN SANDOE BOOKS
21. BENJAMIN POLLOCK'S TOY SHOP
22. GINGER PIG
23. HATCHARDS
24. TWININGS
25. VINTAGE HOUSE
26. VIVIENNE WESTWOOD
27. 45 PARK LANE
28. BOUNDARY
29. CLARIDGE'S FOYER & READING ROOM
30. DUCK & WAFFLE

LONDON

One of the world's most visited cities, London has something for everyone: from history and culture to fine food and good times. Immersed in history, London's rich seams of eye-opening antiquity are everywhere. The city's buildings are striking milestones in a unique and beguiling biography, and a great many of them – the Tower of London, Westminster Abbey, Big Ben – are instantly recognisable landmarks.

① ROYAL ALBERT HALL
www.royalalberthall.com

Built in 1871, thanks in part to the proceeds of the 1851 Great Exhibition, this huge, domed, red-brick amphitheatre, adorned with a frieze of Minton tiles, is Britain's most famous concert venue.

② IMPERIAL WAR MUSEUM
www.iwm.org.uk

Fronted by a pair of intimidating 15in naval guns, this riveting museum is housed in what was the Bethlehem Royal Hospital, a psychiatric hospital also known as Bedlam.

③ WHITECHAPEL GALLERY
www.whitechapelgallery.org

A firm favourite of art students and the avant-garde cognoscenti, this groundbreaking gallery doesn't have a permanent collection but is instead devoted to hosting edgy exhibitions of contemporary art.

④ VIKTOR WYND MUSEUM OF CURIOSITIES, FINE ART & NATURAL HISTORY
www.thelasttuesdaysociety.org

Museum? Art project? Cocktail bar? This is not a venue that's easily classifiable. Inspired by Victorian-era cabinets of curiosities, Wynd's wilfully eccentric collection includes stuffed birds, pickled genitals and two-headed lambs.

⑤ ELFIN OAK

This 900-year-old tree stump is carved with elves, gnomes, witches and small creatures. A photo in the gate-fold of Pink Floyd's *Ummagumma* album has David Gilmour standing in front of the Elfin Oak.

⑥ SPEAKERS' CORNER

Frequented by Karl Marx, Vladimir Lenin, George Orwell and William Morris, Speakers' Corner in the northeastern corner of Hyde Park is traditionally the spot for oratorical acrobatics and soapbox ranting.

⑦ BIG BEN

The most famous feature of the Palace of Westminster is Elizabeth Tower, more commonly known as Big Ben – which is actually the name of the 13.5-tonne bell hanging inside the 315ft tower.

⑧ CHURCHILL WAR ROOMS
www.iwm.org.uk/visits/churchill-war-rooms

Winston Churchill helped coordinate the Allied resistance against Nazi Germany from this underground complex during WWII. The Cabinet War Rooms remain much as they were when the lights were switched off in 1945.

⑨ GEFFRYE MUSEUM
www.geffrye-museum.org.uk

If you like nosing around other people's homes, you'll love this museum devoted to middle-class domestic interiors dating from 1630 to the present day.

⑩ BOROUGH MARKET
www.boroughmarket.org.uk

Located in this spot in some form or another since the 13th century (possibly since 1014), 'London's Larder' has enjoyed an astonishing renaissance, specialising in high-end fresh produce.

⑪ LONDON EYE
www.londoneye.com

Standing 135m high in a fairly flat city, the London Eye affords views 40 km (25 miles) in every direction, weather permitting. Interactive tablets provide great information about landmarks as they appear in the skyline.

⑫ TATE MODERN
www.tate.org.uk

This modern- and contemporary-art gallery is a spellbinding synthesis of modern art and capacious industrial brick design, complete with outdoor viewing platform offering a vista of the city's skyline.

⑬ LAMB & FLAG
www.lambandflagcoventgarden.co.uk

Everybody's favourite pub in central London, pint-sized Lamb & Flag is full of charm and history. Rain or shine, you'll have to elbow your way to the bar.

⑭ SKY POD
www.skygarden.london

One of the best places in the City to get high is the Sky Pod in the Sky Garden on level 35 of the so-called Walkie Talkie building. The views are nothing short of phenomenal.

15 CONNAUGHT BAR
www.the-connaught.co.uk/mayfair-bars/
connaught-bar

Drinkers who know their stuff single out the travelling Martini trolley for particular praise, but almost everything at this sumptuous bar at the exclusive and very British Connaught Hotel gets the nod.

16 RONNIE SCOTT'S
www.ronniescotts.co.uk

Ronnie Scott's jazz club opened at this address in 1965 and became widely known as Britain's best. Support acts are at 7pm, with main gigs at 8.15pm.

17 PRINCE CHARLES CINEMA
www.princecharlescinema.com

As well as new releases, Central London's cheapest cinema hosts Q&As with film directors, sleepover movie marathons and exuberant sing-along screenings of films like *Frozen* and *The Rocky Horror Picture Show*.

18 WIGMORE HALL
www.wigmore-hall.org.uk

This is one of the best and most active classical-music venues in town, with fantastic acoustics, a beautiful art-nouveau hall and a great variety of concerts and recitals.

19 AMUSED MOOSE SOHO
www.amusedmoose.com

One of the city's best clubs, the peripatetic Amused Moose is popular with audiences and comedians alike, perhaps helped along by the fact that heckling is 'unacceptable'.

20 JOHN SANDOE BOOKS
www.johnsandoe.com

The perfect antidote to impersonal book superstores, this atmospheric three-storey bookshop in 18th-century premises is a treasure trove of literary gems and hidden surprises.

21 BENJAMIN POLLOCK'S TOY SHOP
www.pollocks-coventgarden.co.uk

This traditional toy shop is stuffed with Victorian paper theatres, wooden marionettes and finger puppets, and antique teddy bears (that look far too fragile to cuddle much less play with).

22 GINGER PIG
www.thegingerpig.co.uk/shops/moxon-street-london

Arguably one of London's best butchers serves up lunch and picnic fare including sliced meats, pies, sausage rolls and salads.

23 HATCHARDS
www.hatchards.co.uk

London's oldest bookshop dates to 1797. Holding three royal warrants, it's a stupendous bookshop now in the Waterstones stable, and is bursting at its smart seams with very browsable stock.

24 TWININGS
www.twinings.co.uk

This teashop was opened by Thomas Twining in 1706 and is thought to be the oldest company in the capital still trading on the same site. There are free tastings at the tea bar.

25 VINTAGE HOUSE
www.vintagehouse.london

A whisky connoisseur's paradise, this shop stocks more than 1400 single-malt Scotches, from smooth Macallan to peaty Lagavulin. It also offers a huge array of spirits and liqueurs.

26 VIVIENNE WESTWOOD
www.viviennewestwood.com

The designer who created the punk look continues to design clothes as bold, innovative and provocative as ever. In her flagship store you are likely to find 19th-century-inspired bustiers, wedge shoes, tartan and sharp tailoring.

27 45 PARK LANE
www.dorchestercollection.com/en/london/45-park-lane

Part of the upscale Dorchester Collection, this luxurious hotel's address alone is sufficiently evocative as a name, enjoying as it does one of the most prestigious locations in London.

28 BOUNDARY
www.theboundary.co.uk

Each of the 17 rooms and suites in Terence Conran's impressive design hotel takes its theme from a particular designer or design style. It's all very minimalist, even a tad austere.

29 CLARIDGE'S FOYER & READING ROOM
www.claridges.co.uk

Extend that pinkie finger to partake in afternoon tea within the classic art-deco foyer and Reading Room of this landmark hotel.

30 DUCK & WAFFLE
www.duckandwaffle.com

If you like your views with sustenance, this restaurant is the place for you. Perched atop Heron Tower, it serves European and British dishes by day, waffles by night, and round-the-clocktails.

BARCELONA

Barcelona is an enchanting seaside city with boundless culture, fabled architecture and world-class drinking and dining. The sculptural masterpieces of Gaudí and his contemporaries are prevalent throughout the city, and continue to inspire a thriving art scene. The city's architectural treasures span 2000-plus years, the deep blue Mediterranean beckons and the night holds limitless possibilities.

① LA SAGRADA FAMÍLIA
www.sagradafamilia.cat

If you have time for only one sightseeing outing, this is it. The building inspires awe by its sheer verticality and when completed, the highest tower will be half as high again.

② PARK GÜELL
www.parkguell.cat

This open-air space is where Gaudí turned his hand to landscape gardening. It's a strange, enchanting place where the artificial almost seems more natural than the natural.

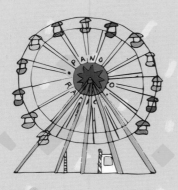

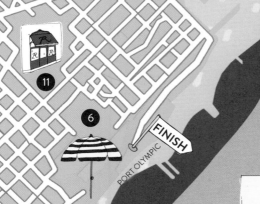

7 EL RAVAL

The once down-and-out district of El Raval is still seedy in parts, though it has seen remarkable rejuvenation in recent years, with the addition of cutting-edge museums and cultural centres.

8 L'EIXAMPLE

The elegant, if traffic-filled district of L'Eixample (pronounced 'lay-sham-pluh') is a showcase for Modernista architecture and art nouveau masterpieces.

9 MONTJUIC

The hillside overlooking the port has some of the city's finest art collections: the Museu Nacional d'Art de Catalunya (MNAC), the Fundació Joan Miró and CaixaForum. Other galleries, gardens and an imposing castle form part of the scenery.

10 TAPAS 24

www.carlesabellan.com/mis-restaurantes/tapas-24

Carles Abellan runs this basement tapas haven known for its gourmet versions of old faves. Specials include a thick black *arròs negre de sípia* (squid-ink black rice).

11 CAN RECASENS

One of Poblenou's most romantic restaurant settings, Can Recasens hides a warren of warmly lit rooms full of oil paintings, flickering candles, fairy lights and baskets of fruit. The food is outstanding.

12 TICKETS

www.ticketsbar.es

A tapas bar opened by Ferran Adrià, of the legendary El Bulli, and his brother Albert. And unlike El Bulli, it's an affordable venture – if you can book a table, that is.

13 LES TOPETTES

www.lestopettes.com

A chic little temple to soap and perfume. The items in this shop's collection have been picked for design as much as product, and you'll find gorgeously packaged scents, candles and unguents.

14 FORMATGERIA LA SEU

www.formatgerialaseu.com

Dedicated to artisan cheeses from all across Spain, this small shop is the antithesis of mass production – it sells only the best from small-scale farmers and the stock changes regularly.

15 AMAPOLA VEGAN SHOP

www.amapolaveganshop.com

Amapola proves that you need not toss your ethics aside in the quest for stylish clothing and accessories. You'll find sleek leather-alternatives for handbags and messenger bags, ballerina-style flats and elegant scarves.

3 MUSEU PICASSO

www.museupicasso.bcn.cat

The setting alone, in five contiguous medieval stone mansions, makes the museum unique. The pretty courtyards, galleries and staircases preserved in the first three buildings are as delightful as the collection inside.

4 MERCAT DE LA BOQUERIA

www.boqueria.info

Mercat de la Boqueria is possibly La Rambla's most interesting building, not so much for its Modernista-influenced design, but for the action of the food market within.

5 CAMP NOU EXPERIENCE

www.fcbarcelona.com

A pilgrimage site for football fans, Camp Nou is one of Barcelona's most hallowed grounds. Nothing compares to attending a live match, and the experience is a must for FC Barcelona fans.

6 PLATJES

A series of pleasant beaches stretches northeast from the Port Olímpic marina. They are largely artificial, but this doesn't stop an estimated seven million bathers from piling in every year!

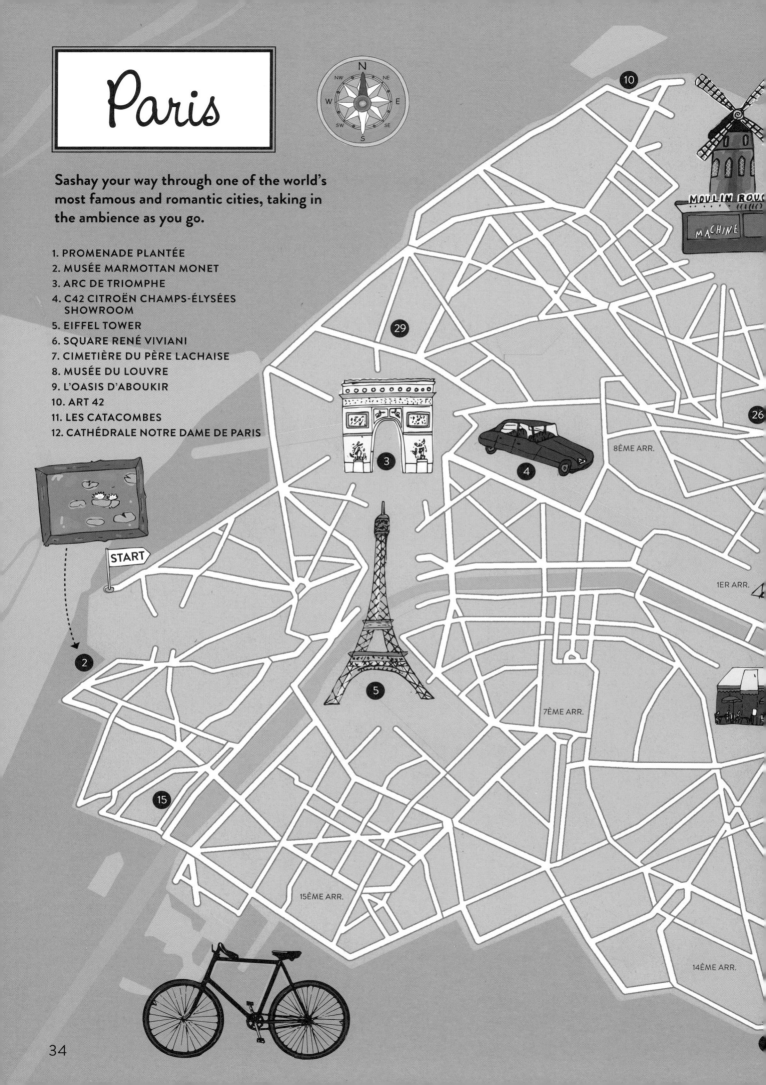

Paris

Sashay your way through one of the world's most famous and romantic cities, taking in the ambience as you go.

1. PROMENADE PLANTÉE
2. MUSÉE MARMOTTAN MONET
3. ARC DE TRIOMPHE
4. C42 CITROËN CHAMPS-ÉLYSÉES SHOWROOM
5. EIFFEL TOWER
6. SQUARE RENÉ VIVIANI
7. CIMETIÈRE DU PÈRE LACHAISE
8. MUSÉE DU LOUVRE
9. L'OASIS D'ABOUKIR
10. ART 42
11. LES CATACOMBES
12. CATHÉDRALE NOTRE DAME DE PARIS

START

MOULIN ROUGE
MACHINE

8ÈME ARR.

1ER ARR.

7ÈME ARR.

15ÈME ARR.

14ÈME ARR.

9ÈME ARR.

10ÈME ARR.

2ÈME ARR.

11ÈME ARR.

FINISH

13. MAMA SHELTER
14. HÔTEL EXQUIS
15. HÔTEL FÉLICIEN
16. RESTAURANT AT
17. BOUILLON RACINE
18. BERTHILLON
19. LE BARON ROUGE
20. LES DEUX MAGOTS
21. OPÉRA BASTILLE

22. CAFÉ UNIVERSEL
23. MOULIN ROUGE
24. PHILHARMONIE DE PARIS
25. THÉÂTRE DU LUXEMBOURG
26. GALERIES LAFAYETTE
27. LE BONBON AU PALAIS
28. SHAKESPEARE & COMPANY
29. FROMAGERIE ALLÉOSSE
30. MARCHÉ AUX PUCES DE ST-OUEN

Paris

Paris has a timeless familiarity for first-time and frequent visitors, with instantly recognisable architectural icons, along with exquisite cuisine, chic boutiques and priceless artistic treasures. The wrought-iron spire of the Eiffel Tower, the broad Arc de Triomphe guarding the city's most glamorous avenue, the Champs-Élysées, and the gargoyled Notre Dame cathedral are indelibly etched in the minds of anyone who's visited the city.

① PROMENADE PLANTÉE

The disued 19th-century Vincennes railway viaduct was reborn as the world's first elevated park, planted with a fragrant profusion of cherry trees, maples, rose trellises, bamboo corridors and lavender.

② MUSÉE MARMOTTAN MONET
www.marmottan.fr

This museum showcases the world's largest collection of works by impressionist painter Claude Monet – about a hundred – as well as paintings by Gauguin, Sisley, Pissarro, Renoir, Degas, Manet and Berthe Morisot.

③ ARC DE TRIOMPHE
www.paris-arc-de-triomphe.fr

If anything rivals the Eiffel Tower as the symbol of Paris, it's this magnificent 1836 monument to Napoléon's victory at Austerlitz (1805).

④ C42 CITROËN CHAMPS-ÉLYSÉES SHOWROOM
www.citroen.fr

C42 is unlike any other car showroom. Fresh-off-the-drawing-board vehicles are stacked on a huge hydraulic tower, while amusements include table football, ping-pong and an 'escape room' game.

⑤ EIFFEL TOWER
www.toureiffel.paris

No one could imagine Paris today without it. But Gustave Eiffel constructed this elegant, 320m-tall signature spire as a temporary exhibit for the 1889 World's Fair. Luckily, the tower's popularity assured its survival.

⑥ SQUARE RENÉ VIVIANI

This picturesque little park is home to the oldest tree in Paris. The black locust was planted in 1602 by Henri III, Henri IV and Louis XII's gardener, Jean Robin.

⑦ CIMETIÈRE DU PÈRE LACHAISE
www.pere-lachaise.com

The world's most-visited cemetery opened in 1804. Its 70,000 ornate and ostentatious tombs of the rich and famous form a verdant, 110-acre sculpture garden.

⑧ MUSÉE DU LOUVRE
www.louvre.fr

Paris' pièce de résistance and the world's most-visited museum showcases 35,000 works of art; it would take nine months to glance at every piece.

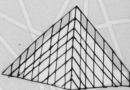

⑨ L'OASIS D'ABOUKIR

This extraordinary *mur végétal* ('vertical garden') was installed on a 25m-high blank building façade and incorporates some 7600 different plants from 237 different species.

⑩ ART 42
www.art42.fr

Street art and post-graffiti now have their own dedicated space at this 'anti-museum' featuring works by Banksy, Bom.K, Miss Van, Ericailcane and Invader, among others.

⑪ LES CATACOMBES
www.catacombes.paris.fr

Paris' most macabre sight are these underground tunnels lined with skulls and bones. In 1785 the bones were exhumed from overflowing cemeteries and stored here; the Catacombes were created in 1810.

⑫ CATHÉDRALE NOTRE DAME DE PARIS
www.notredamedeparis.fr

The city's most visited unticketed site, with upwards of 14 million visitors per year, is a masterpiece of French Gothic architecture. Highlights include its three spectacular rose windows, treasury and bell towers.

⑬ MAMA SHELTER
www.mamashelter.com

This former car park was coaxed into its current zany incarnation by uber-designer Philippe Starck. This hotel's 170 cutting-edge rooms feature iMacs, catchy colour schemes, polished-concrete walls and free movies on demand.

⑭ HÔTEL EXQUIS
www.hotelexquisparis.com

Surrealism is the theme of this excellent-value, three-star hotel. A unique work of surrealist art decorates each room, where designer lighting and bathrooms with twinkling tile lights woo guests.

15 HÔTEL FÉLICIEN
www.hotelfelicienparis.com

Exquisitely designed rooms at this chic boutique hotel, squirrelled away in a 1930s building, feel more five-star than four, with suites more than satisfying their promise of indulgent cocooning.

16 RESTAURANT AT
www.atsushitanaka.com

Chef Atsushi Tanaka showcases abstract artlike masterpieces incorporating unusual ingredients on stunning outsized plates in a blank-canvas-style dining space.

17 BOUILLON RACINE
www.bouillonracine.com

Inconspicuously situated in a quiet street, this heritage-listed art-nouveau 'soup kitchen' was built in 1906 to feed market workers. The food – inspired by age-old recipes – is superbly executed.

18 BERTHILLON
www.berthillon.fr

This esteemed *glacier* (ice-cream maker) offers up 70-plus all-natural, chemical-free flavours, including fruit sorbets and richer ice creams made from fresh milk and eggs.

19 LE BARON ROUGE
www.lebaronrouge.net

Just about the ultimate Parisian wine-bar experience, this wonderfully unpretentious local meeting place where everyone is welcome has barrels stacked against the bottle-lined walls and serves cheese, charcuterie and oysters.

20 LES DEUX MAGOTS
www.lesdeuxmagots.fr

If ever there was a cafe that summed up St-Germain des Prés' early-20th-century literary scene, it's this former hangout of anyone who was anyone.

21 OPÉRA BASTILLE
www.operadeparis.fr

Paris' premier opera hall, Opéra Bastille's 2745-seat main auditorium also stages ballet and classical concerts. Standing-only tickets (*places débouts*) are available 90 minutes before performances.

22 CAFÉ UNIVERSEL
www.cafeuniversel.com

Café Universel hosts a brilliant array of live concerts, with everything from bebop and Latin sounds to vocal jazz sessions, in a convivial relaxed atmosphere.

23 MOULIN ROUGE
www.moulinrouge.fr

Immortalised in Toulouse-Lautrec's posters, Paris's legendary cabaret twinkles beneath a 1925 replica of its original red windmill. Shows here are a whirl of fantastical costumes, sets, choreography and Champagne.

24 PHILHARMONIE DE PARIS
http://philharmoniedeparis.fr

Philharmonie de Paris hosts an eclectic range of concerts – from classical to North African and Japanese – in the 2015-inaugurated Grande Salle Pierre Boulez.

25 THÉÂTRE DU LUXEMBOURG
www.marionnettesduluxembourg.fr

You don't have to be a kid or be able to speak French to be delighted by marionette shows, which have entertained audiences in France since the Middle Ages.

26 GALERIES LAFAYETTE
www.haussmann.galerieslafayette.com

Grande-dame department store Galeries Lafayette is spread across the main store (whose magnificent stained-glass dome is over a century old), men's store and homewares store, with a gourmet emporium.

27 LE BONBON AU PALAIS
www.bonbonsaupalais.fr

Kids and kids-at-heart will adore this sugar-fuelled tour de France. The school-geography-themed boutique stocks rainbows of artisan sweets from around the country.

28 SHAKESPEARE & COMPANY
www.shakespeareandcompany.com

Shakespeare's enchanting nooks and crannies overflow with new and secondhand English-language books. The original shop was run by Sylvia Beach and became the meeting point for Hemingway's 'Lost Generation'.

29 FROMAGERIE ALLÉOSSE
www.fromage-alleosse.com

Alléosse is the city's only fromagerie with its own cheese-ripening *caves* (cellars) spanning 300 sq metres, with four separate environments. Its 250-plus cheeses are grouped into five main categories.

30 MARCHÉ AUX PUCES DE ST-OUEN
www.marcheauxpuces-saintouen.com

This vast flea market, founded in the late 19th century and said to be Europe's largest, has more than 2500 stalls grouped into 15 *marchés* (markets), each with its own speciality.

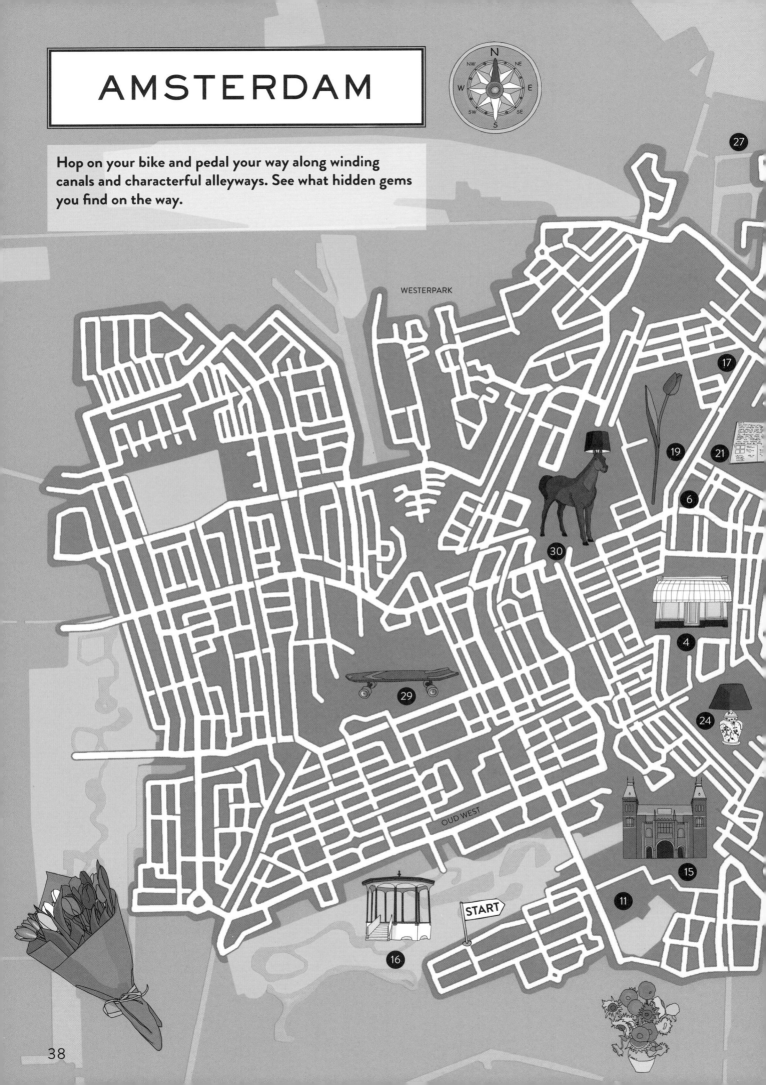

AMSTERDAM

Hop on your bike and pedal your way along winding canals and characterful alleyways. See what hidden gems you find on the way.

WESTERPARK

OUD WEST

START

1. BLOEMENMARKET
2. HERMITAGE AMSTERDAM
3. HET SCHEEPVAARTMUSEUM
4. WESTERN CANAL RING
5. OUDE KERK
6. HOMOMONUMENT
7. VLEMINCKX
8. BROUWERIJ 'T IJ
9. ARCAM
10. ALBERT CUYPMARKET
11. VAN GOGH MUSEUM
12. CENTRALE BIBLIOTHEEK
13. ROYAL PALACE
14. BEGIJNHOF
15. RIJKSMUSEUM
16. VONDELPARK
17. WINKEL 43
18. HEINEKEN EXPERIENCE BREWERY
19. AMSTERDAM TULIP MUSEUM
20. BITTERZOET
21. ANNE FRANK HUIS MUSEUM
22. COCOMAMA
23. HOUSEBOAT MS LUCTOR
24. SEVEN ONE SEVEN LUXURY HOTEL
25. DAM
26. BUFFET VAN ODETTE
27. MARIUS
28. WATERLOOPLEIN FLEA MARKET
29. LOCAL GOODS STORE
30. MOOOI GALLERY

NOORD

FINISH

CENTRUM

DE PIJP

DE PLANTAGE

39

AMSTERDAM

Golden Age canals lined by tilting gabled buildings are the backdrop for Amsterdam's treasure-packed museums, vintage-filled shops and hyper-creative art and design, drinking, dining and crazy clubbing scenes. There's a sense of time stopping, an intimacy of the here-and-now that leaves your troubles behind, at least until tomorrow.

1 BLOEMENMARKET

One of the world's most famous flower markets, the canalside Bloemenmarket has been here since the 1860s, when gardeners used to sail up the Amstel and sell from their boats.

2 HERMITAGE AMSTERDAM

The long-standing ties of Russia and the Netherlands led to this local branch of St Petersburg's State Hermitage Museum. Blockbuster temporary exhibitions, such as treasures from the Russian palace or masterworks by Matisse and Picasso, change about twice per year.

3 HET SCHEEPVAARTMUSEUM

An immense, 17th-century admiralty building houses one of the world's most extensive collections of maritime memorabilia. Early shipping routes, naval combat, fishing and whaling are all detailed, and there are some 500 models of boats and ships.

4 WESTERN CANAL RING

One of Amsterdam's most gorgeous areas. Grand old mansions and oddball little specialty shops line the glinting waterways. Roaming around them can cause entire days to vanish.

5 OUDE KERK

This is Amsterdam's oldest surviving building (from 1306). It's also an intriguing moral contradiction: a church surrounded by active Red Light District windows. Inside, check out the stunning Müller organ, the naughty 15th-century carvings on the choir stalls and famous Amsterdammers' tombstones in the floor.

6 HOMOMONUMENT

Behind the Westerkerk, this 1987 cluster of three 10 x 10 x 10-metre granite triangles recalls persecution by the Nazis, who forced gay men to wear a pink triangle patch. One of the triangles steps down into the Keizersgracht and is said to represent a jetty from which gay men were sent to the concentration camps.

7 VLEMINCKX

Vleminckx has been frying up *frites* (French fries) since 1887, and doing it at this hole-in-the-wall takeaway shack near the Spui for more than 50 years. The standard is smothered in mayonnaise, though you can also ask for ketchup, peanut sauce or a variety of spicy toppings.

8 BROUWERIJ 'T IJ
www.brouwerijhetij.nl

Beneath the creaking sails of the 1725-built De Gooyer windmill, Amsterdam's leading organic microbrewery produces delicious (and often very potent) standard, seasonal and limited-edition brews. Pop in for a beer in the tiled tasting room, lined by an amazing bottle collection, or on the plane tree-shaded terrace.

9 ARCAM

This showpiece building of the Amsterdam Architecture Foundation is a one-stop shop for all your architectural needs. Expert staff are on hand to interpret the fascinating changing exhibits, and you can find books, guide maps and suggestions for tours on foot, by bike and by public transport.

10 ALBERT CUYPMARKET

The half-mile-long Albert Cuypmarket is Amsterdam's largest, busiest market. Here immigrants mix with locals, hawking rice cookers, spices and Dutch snacks such as herring sandwiches. Graze as you gaze on the goods on offer.

11 VAN GOGH MUSEUM
www.vangoghmuseum.com

It's a moving experience to visit this museum, which traces the artist's life via the world's largest Van Gogh collection, with many of his most famous masterworks, plus wonderful little-known pieces.

12 CENTRALE BIBLIOTHEEK

This symmetrical, nine-storey 'tower of knowledge' (its self-appointed nickname) is the country's largest library. Unveiled in 2007, it has claimed a commanding spot in Amsterdam's increasingly modern landscape.

13 ROYAL PALACE

Opened as a town hall in 1655, this building became a palace in the 19th century. The interiors gleam, especially the marble work – at its best in a floor inlaid with maps of the world in the great *burgerzaal* (citizens' hall), which occupies the heart of the building.

(14) BEGIJNHOF
www.nicolaas-parochie.nl

This enclosed former convent dates from the early 14th century. It's a surreal oasis of peace, with tiny houses and postage-stamp gardens around a well-kept courtyard.

(15) RIJKSMUSEUM
www.rijksmuseum.nl

The Rijksmuseum is the Netherlands' premier art trove, splashing Rembrandts, Vermeers and 7500 other masterpieces over 1.5km of galleries. Rembrandt's *The Night Watch* (1642) takes pride of place.

(16) VONDELPARK
www.hetvondelpark.net

The lush urban idyll of the Vondelpark is one of Amsterdam's most magical places – sprawling, English-style gardens, with ponds, lawns, footbridges and winding footpaths. On a sunny day, an open-air party atmosphere ensues.

(17) WINKEL 43

This sprawling, indoor-outdoor space is great for people-watching, popular for coffees and small meals, and out-of-the-park for its tall, cakey apple pie. On market days (Monday and Saturday) there's almost always a queue out the door.

(18) HEINEKEN EXPERIENCE BREWERY
www.heineken.com

On the site of the company's old brewery, the crowning glory of this self-guided 'Experience' (samples aside) is a multimedia exhibit where you 'become' a beer (shaken up, sprayed and heated).

(19) AMSTERDAM TULIP MUSEUM
www.amsterdamtulipmuseum.com

Don't be distracted by the gift shop overflowing with floral souvenirs, and yes, it is small, but this museum offers a nifty overview of the history of the country's favourite bloom.

(20) BITTERZOET
www.bitterzoet.com

Always full, always changing, this venue with a capacity of just 350 people is one of the friendliest places in town, with a diverse crowd. Music (sometimes live, sometimes courtesy of a DJ) can be funk, roots, drum 'n' bass, Latin, Afro-beat, old-school jazz or hip-hop groove.

(21) ANNE FRANK HUIS MUSEUM
www.annefrank.org

With its reconstruction of Anne Frank's melancholy bedroom and her actual diary – sitting alone in its glass case, filled with sunnily optimistic writing tempered by quiet despair – this museum is a powerful experience.

(22) COCOMAMA
www.cocomama.nl

Amsterdam's first self-proclaimed 'boutique hostel' plays up its salacious past (the building was home to a high-end brothel) in some bunk rooms, while others are more demure, with Delftware or windmill themes.

(23) HOUSEBOAT MS LUCTOR
www.boatbedandbreakfast.nl

A brimming organic breakfast basket is delivered to you each morning at this self-contained mahogany-panelled 1913 houseboat bed and breakfast, moored in a quiet waterway 10 minutes' walk from Centraal Station.

(24) SEVEN ONE SEVEN LUXURY HOTEL
www.717hotel.nl

The nine hyperplush, deliciously appointed rooms at this hotel come with that all-too-rare luxury in this city: space. Step into the prodigious Picasso suite – with its soaring ceiling, elongated sofa and contemporary and antique decorations – and you may never, ever want to leave.

(25) DAM

This square is the very spot where Amsterdam was founded around 1270. Today, pigeons, tourists, buskers and the occasional funfair complete with Ferris wheel take over the grounds. It's still a national gathering spot, and if there's a major speech or demonstration, it is held here.

(26) BUFFET VAN ODETTE
www.buffetvanodette.nl

Not a buffet, but an airy, white-tiled, sit-down cafe with a beautiful canal-side terrace, where Odette shows how good simple cooking can taste when you start with great ingredients and creativity.

(27) MARIUS
www.deworst.nl

Foodies swoon over the pocket-sized Marius restaurant, tucked in amid artists' studios in the Western Islands. Chef Kees Elfring shops at local markets, then creates his daily four-course, no-choice menu from what he finds.

(28) WATERLOOPLEIN FLEA MARKET
www.waterlooplein.amsterdam

Covering the square once known as Vlooienburg (Flea Town), the Waterlooplein Flea Market draws bargain hunters seeking everything from antique knick-knacks to vintage leather coats.

(29) LOCAL GOODS STORE
www.awesomeamsterdam.com/local-goods-store

As the name implies, everything at this concept shop inside De Hallen is created by Dutch designers. Look for skateboards, gin-production kits, purses, wooden bow ties, hand-dyed scarves and more.

(30) MOOOI GALLERY
www.moooi.com

This is Dutch design at its most over-the-top, from the life-sized black horse lamp to the 'killing of the piggy bank' ceramic pig (with a gold hammer).

ROME

Rome is a historic gem of a city. Find your way through its ancient streets from the south to the north.

CAMPO MARZIO

20

13

21

CITTA DEL VATICANO

BORGO

12

6

5

PARIONE

29

TRASTEVERE

28

MONTEVERDE

TESTACCIO

START

1. COLOSSEUM
2. CAPITOLINE MUSEUMS
3. PALATINO
4. ROMAN FORUM
5. PANTHEON
6. PIAZZA NAVONA
7. BASILICA DI SANTA MARIA MAGGIORE
8. BASILICA DI SAN GIOVANNI IN LATERANO
9. WISHLIST
10. VIA APPIA ANTICA

11. TREVI FOUNTAIN
12. ST PETER'S BASILICA
13. VATICAN MUSEUMS
14. INN AT THE ROMAN FORUM
15. GENERATOR HOSTEL
16. PANELLA
17. SBANCO
18. COLLINE EMILIANE
19. CAFFÈ GRECO
20. SCIASCIA CAFFÈ

21. BE.RE
22. IL SORÌ
23. TEATRO DELL'OPERA DI ROMA
24. TERME DI CARACALLA
25. CAFFÈ LETTERARIO
26. NUOVO CINEMA PALAZZO
27. CONFETTERIA MORIONDO & GARIGLIO
28. ANTICA CACIARA TRASTEVERINA
29. BENHEART
30. FAUSTO SANTINI

FINISH

LUDOVISI

CASTRO
PRETORIO

ESQUILINO

SAN
GIOVANNI

RIPA

ROME

A heady mix of haunting ruins, awe-inspiring art and vibrant street life, Italy's hot-blooded capital is one of the world's most romantic and inspiring cities. A trip to Rome is as much about lapping up the *dolce vita* lifestyle as gorging on art and culture. Idling around picturesque streets, whiling away hours at streetside cafes, people-watching on pretty piazzas – these are all an integral part of the Roman experience.

① COLOSSEUM
www.coopculture.it

Rome's great gladiatorial arena is the most thrilling of the city's ancient sights. Inaugurated in AD 80, the 50,000-seat Colosseum was recently given a major clean-up, the first in its 2000-year history.

② CAPITOLINE MUSEUMS
www.museicapitolini.org

Dating to 1471, the Capitoline Museums are the world's oldest public museum. Their collection of classical sculpture is one of Italy's finest, including crowd-pleasers such as the iconic *Lupa Capitolina* (Capitoline Wolf).

③ PALATINO
www.coopculture.it

An atmospheric area of pine trees, majestic ruins and memorable views, it was here that Romulus supposedly founded the city in 753 BC and Rome's emperors lived in unabashed luxury.

④ ROMAN FORUM
www.coopculture.it

Ancient Rome's showpiece centre, this grandiose district of temples, basilicas and vibrant public spaces was first developed in the 7th century BC and eventually became the social, political and commercial hub of the empire.

⑤ PANTHEON
www.pantheonroma.com

A striking 2000-year-old temple, now a church, the Pantheon is the best preserved of Rome's ancient monuments and one of the most influential buildings in the Western world.

⑥ PIAZZA NAVONA

With its showy fountains, baroque palazzi (mansions) and colourful cast of street artists, hawkers and tourists, Piazza Navona is central Rome's elegant showcase square.

⑦ BASILICA DI SANTA MARIA MAGGIORE

One of Rome's four patriarchal basilicas, this monumental 5th-century church stands on the summit of the Esquiline Hill, on the spot where snow is said to have miraculously fallen in the summer of AD 358.

⑧ BASILICA DI SAN GIOVANNI IN LATERANO

For a thousand years this monumental cathedral was the most important church in Christendom. Commissioned by Constantine and consecrated in AD 324, it was the first Christian basilica built in the city.

⑨ WISHLIST
www.facebook.com/wishlistclub

A black door marks the entrance to this eternally popular music club, in a low-lying building on one of San Lorenzo's grungiest streets. Gigs cover all sounds.

⑩ VIA APPIA ANTICA
www.parcoappiaantica.it

Via Appia Antica has long been one of Rome's most exclusive addresses, a beautiful cobbled thoroughfare flanked by grassy fields, Roman structures and towering pine trees.

⑪ TREVI FOUNTAIN

A flamboyant baroque ensemble of mythical figures and wild horses, the tradition here is to toss a coin into the water, ensuring that you'll return to Rome.

⑫ ST PETER'S BASILICA
www.vatican.va

In this city of outstanding churches, none can hold a candle to St Peter's, Italy's largest, richest and most spectacular basilica. It was consecrated in 1626 after 120 years' construction.

⑬ VATICAN MUSEUMS
www.museivaticani.va

Founded by Pope Julius II in the early 16th century and enlarged by successive pontiffs, the Vatican Museums boast one of the world's greatest art collections. Highlights include the Michelangelo-painted Sistine Chapel.

⑭ INN AT THE ROMAN FORUM
www.theinnattheromanforum.com

Hidden behind a discreet entrance in a quiet street near the Imperial Forums, this chic boutique hotel is pure gold, from the friendly welcome to the contemporary-styled rooms and panoramic roof terrace.

(15) GENERATOR HOSTEL
www.generatorhostels.com

This designer hostel is, quite frankly, more uber-cool hotel in mood – 72% of the 174 beds here are in bright white private rooms, and dorms max out at four beds.

(16) PANELLA
www.panellaroma.com

This enticing bakery is littered with well-used baking trays of freshly baked pastries loaded with confectioner's custard, wild-cherry fruit tartlets, *pizza al taglio*, *arancini* and focaccia.

(17) SBANCO

With its informal warehouse vibe and buzzing atmosphere, Sbanco is one of the capital's hottest pizzerias, serving up creative, wood-fired pizzas and sumptuous fried starters.

(18) COLLINE EMILIANE
www.collineemiliane.com

Sensational regional cuisine from Emilia-Romagna aside, what makes this small white-tablecloth dining address so outstanding is its family vibe and overwhelmingly warm service.

(19) CAFFÈ GRECO

Rome's oldest cafe, open since 1760, is still working the look with the utmost elegance: waiters in black tails and bow tie, waitresses in frilly white pinnies, scarlet flock walls and age-spotted gilt mirrors.

(20) SCIASCIA CAFFÈ

Nothing tops the *caffè eccellente* served at this polished old-school cafe. A velvety smooth espresso served in a delicate cup lined with melted chocolate, it's nothing short of magnificent.

(21) BE.RE
www.be-re.eu

With its copper beer taps, exposed brick decor and high vaulted ceilings, this contemporary bar is a good-looking spot for an evening of Italian beers and cask ales.

(22) IL SORÌ
www.ilsori.it

Every last salami slice and chunk of cheese has been carefully selected from Italy's finest artisanal and small producers at this gourmet wine bar and bottega.

(23) TEATRO DELL'OPERA DI ROMA
www.operaroma.it

Rome's premier opera house boasts a plush gilt interior, a Fascist 1920s exterior and an impressive history: it premiered Puccini's *Tosca*, and Maria Callas once sang here.

(24) TERME DI CARACALLA
www.operaroma.it

The hulking ruins of this vast 3rd-century baths complex set the memorable stage for the Teatro dell'Opera's summer season of music, opera and ballet, as well as shows by big-name Italian performers.

(25) CAFFÈ LETTERARIO
www.caffeletterarioroma.it

An intellectual hangout housed in the funky post-industrial space of a former garage. With a bookshop, gallery, co-working space and lounge bar, performances range from soul and jazz to Indian dance.

(26) NUOVO CINEMA PALAZZO
www.nuovocinemapalazzo.it

Features a bevy of exciting creative happenings: think film screenings, theatre performances, DJ sets, concerts, live music, break dance classes and a host of other artsy events.

(27) CONFETTERIA MORIONDO & GARIGLIO

Roman poet Trilussa was so smitten with this historic chocolate shop that he was moved to mention it in verse. Delicious handmade chocolates, many prepared according to original 19th-century recipes.

(28) ANTICA CACIARA TRASTEVERINA
www.anticacaciara.it

The fresh ricotta is a prized possession at this century-old deli, and it's all usually snapped up by lunchtime. If you're too late, take solace in the to-die-for *ricotta infornata* (oven-baked ricotta).

(29) BENHEART
www.benheart.it

Everything about this artisanal leather boutique is achingly cool. Benheart is one of Italy's savviest talents, and his fashionable handmade shoes and jackets for men and women are glorious.

(30) FAUSTO SANTINI
www.faustosantini.com

Rome's best-known shoe designer, Fausto Santini, is famous for his beguilingly simple, architectural shoe designs, with beautiful boots and shoes made from butter-soft leather.

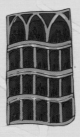

COPENHAGEN

Copenhagen is the epitome of Scandi cool. From Viking treasures to iconic Danish chairs and hip streetwear, the city's cultural offerings are rich and eclectic. Bridges buzz with cycling commuters and locals dive into pristine waterways; it's Copenhagen's simplicity that creates a quiet sense of delight.

① TIVOLI GARDENS
www.tivoli.dk

Dating from 1843, tasteful Tivoli wins fans with its dreamy whirl of amusement rides, twinkling pavilions, carnival games and open-air stage shows. Ride the century-old rollercoaster and enjoy the Saturday fireworks display.

② CHRISTIANIA

Escape the capitalist crunch at Freetown Christiania, a dreadlocks-heavy commune straddling the eastern side of Christianshavn. Established in 1971, the area houses collective businesses, workshops and communal living.

5 JENS OLSEN'S WORLD CLOCK

Climb the 300 steps to see the clock designed by astromechanic Jens Olsen (1872–1945), displaying not only the local time, but sunrises, sunsets and planet revolutions.

6 URBAN HOUSE

www.urbanhouse.me

This huge hostel encompasses three historic buildings in hip Vesterbro. Step in and instantly pick up on the vibe: a vast sitting room with comfy chairs, plus bar with snacks.

7 NYHAVN

There are few nicer places to be on a sunny day than sitting at the outdoor tables of a cafe on the quayside of the Nyhavn canal. The canal was long a haunt for sailors and writers, including Hans Christian Andersen.

8 LILLIAN'S SMØRREBRØD

www.facebook.com/lillianssmorrebrod

One of the best, the oldest (dating from 1978) and least costly *smørrebrød* (open sandwich on rye bread) places, but the word is out, so you may have to opt for a takeaway.

9 NOMA

www.noma.dk

A Holy Grail restaurant for gastronomes across the globe, head chef René Redzepi creates extraordinary symphonies of flavour and texture using Scandinavian-sourced produce.

10 KLASSIK MODERNE MØBELKUNST

www.klassik.dk

A veritable museum of Scandinavian furniture from the mid-20th century, with classics from greats like Poul Henningsen, Hans J Wegner and Nanna Ditzel.

11 POP CPH

www.popcph.dk

In 2005, Mikkel Kristensen and Kasper Henriksen began hosting parties for Copenhagen's creative community, which continue to inspire the duo's burgeoning fashion label.

12 MOTHER RESTAURANT

www.mother.dk

Pizzeria Mother ditches gingham tablecloths for sexy concrete floors, industrial tiles and an X-factor *Kødbyen* (Meat City) address.

13 ILLUMS BOLIGHUS INTERNATIONAL

www.illumsbolighus.dk

Revamp everything from your wardrobe to your living room at this multilevel department store, dedicated to big names in Danish and international design.

14 RADISSON BLU ROYAL HOTEL

This Arne Jacobsen-designed hotel offers guests free Wi-Fi, amazing city views and access to a 2000 sq m state-of-the-art fitness centre.

15 CHRISTIANSHAVN

The setting for parts of the novel and movie *Miss Smilla's Feeling for Snow*, Christianshavn channels Amsterdam with its glittering canals, outdoor cafes and easy-going attitude.

3 ROSENBORG SLOT

www.kongernessamling.dk/en/rosenborg

A 'once-upon-a-time' castle of turrets, gables and a moat, the early-17th-century Rosenborg Slot's 24 upper rooms house the furnishings and portraits of each monarch from Christian IV to Frederik VII.

4 DAVIDS SAMLING

www.davidmus.dk

A wonderful curiosity of a gallery housing Scandinavia's largest collection of Islamic art, and exquisite works of Egyptian, Indian, Dutch, English and French art.

Berlin

Take a historic journey from west to east through this bohemian metropolis, and marvel at the art and culture on offer along the way.

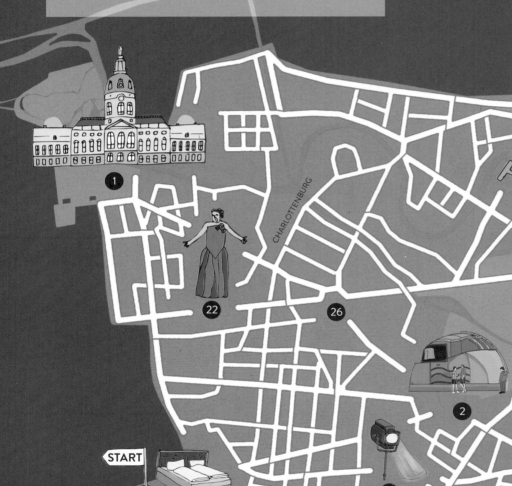

START

CHARLOTTENBURG

MOABIT

SCHONEBERG

1. SCHLOSS CHARLOTTENBURG
2. WELTBRUNNEN
3. COMPUTERSPIELEMUSEUM
4. EAST SIDE GALLERY
5. BRANDENBURGER TOR
6. HOLOCAUST MEMORIAL
7. REICHSTAG
8. KÖNIG GALERIE @ ST AGNES KIRCHE
9. MUSEUMSINSEL
10. BERLINER DOM
11. BUCHSTABENMUSEUM
12. MUSEUM DER UNERHÖRTEN DINGE
13. LOUISA'S PLACE
14. HOTEL ADLON KEMPINSKI
15. AUGUSTINER AM GENDARMENMARKT

16. KOPPS
17. BERGHAIN/PANORAMA BAR
18. ANKERKLAUSE
19. LUFTGARTEN
20. ZUM STARKEN AUGUST
21. BAR JEDER VERNUNFT
22. DEUTSCHE OPER BERLIN
23. FREILUFTKINO FRIEDRICHSHAIN

24. HEBBEL AM UFER
25. BEARPIT KARAOKE
26. MANUFACTUM
27. DUSSMANN – DAS KULTURKAUFHAUS
28. RAUSCH SCHOKOLADENHAUS
29. MARKTHALLE NEUN
30. LP12 MALL OF BERLIN

PRENZLAUER BERG

FRIEDRICHSHAIN

MITTE

KREUZBERG

FINISH

49

Berlin

Berlin's combination of glamour and grit is bound to mesmerise anyone keen to explore its vibrant culture, cutting-edge architecture, fabulous food, intense parties and tangible history. Berlin is a multicultural metropolis, but, deep down, it retains the unpretentious charm of an international village.

(1) SCHLOSS CHARLOTTENBURG
www.spsg.de

This palace is one of the few sites in Berlin that reflects the one-time grandeur of the Hohenzollern clan. An exquisite baroque pile with festival halls and paintings by French 18th-century masters.

(2) WELTBRUNNEN

Everyone from buskers to skateboarding teens gathers around the quirky Weltbrunnen fountain, a creation of Joachim Schmettau. Made from red granite and bronze, it's festooned with sculptures of humans and animals.

(3) COMPUTERSPIELEMUSEUM
www.computerspielemuseum.de

This well-curated museum takes you on a fascinating trip down computer-game memory lane while putting the industry's evolution into historical and cultural context.

(4) EAST SIDE GALLERY
www.eastsidegallery-berlin.de

In 1989 the Berlin Wall, that grim and grey divider of humanity, finally met its maker. Most of it was quickly dismantled, but a 1.3km (0.8 mile) stretch became the world's largest open-air mural collection.

(5) BRANDENBURGER TOR

A symbol of division during the Cold War, the landmark Brandenburg Gate now epitomises German reunification. It stands sentinel over Pariser Platz.

(6) HOLOCAUST MEMORIAL
www.stiftung-denkmal.de

Inaugurated in 2005, this football-field-sized memorial by American architect Peter Eisenman consists of 2711 sarcophagi-like concrete columns rising in sombre silence from undulating ground.

(7) REICHSTAG
www.bundestag.de

It's been burned, bombed, rebuilt, buttressed by the Wall, wrapped in fabric and finally turned into the modern home of the German parliament: the 1894 Reichstag is indeed one of Berlin's most iconic buildings.

(8) KÖNIG GALERIE @ ST AGNES KIRCHE
www.koeniggalerie.com

If art is your religion, a pilgrimage to this church-turned-gallery is a must. In 2012, this decommissioned Catholic church was converted into a spectacular space that presents interdisciplinary, concept-oriented and space-based art.

(9) MUSEUMSINSEL
www.smb.museum

Walk through ancient Babylon, meet an Egyptian queen or be mesmerised by Monet's ethereal landscapes. Welcome to Berlin's most important treasure trove, spread across five grand museums on an island in the Spree.

(10) BERLINER DOM
www.berlinerdom.de

Pompous yet majestic, the Italian Renaissance-style former royal court church (1905) does triple duty as house of worship, museum and concert hall. Inside it's gilt to the hilt.

(11) BUCHSTABENMUSEUM
www.buchstabenmuseum.de

A must for fans of quirky museums, this nonprofit collection in a former supermarket is entirely dedicated to letters of the alphabet.

(12) MUSEUM DER UNERHÖRTEN DINGE
www.museumderunerhoertendinge.de

'Every object tells a story' could be the motto of this kooky collection of curiosities. It may all be a mind-bending spoof, but one thing's certain: it will challenge the way you look at museums.

(13) LOUISA'S PLACE
www.louisas-place.de

The all-suite Louisa's, in a charismatic 1904 building, is the kind of hotel that dazzles with class not glitz. The family-friendly suites brim with individual character, elegant furnishings and full kitchens.

(14) HOTEL ADLON KEMPINSKI
www.kempinski.com

The Adlon has been Berlin's most high-profile defender of the grand tradition since 1907. The striking lobby is a mere overture to the full symphony of luxury awaiting in spacious, amenity-laden rooms.

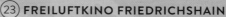

15 AUGUSTINER AM GENDARMENMARKT
www.augustiner-braeu-berlin.de

Tourists, concert-goers and hearty-food lovers rub shoulders at rustic tables in this authentic Bavarian beer hall. Soak up the down-to-earth vibe right along with a mug of full-bodied Augustiner brew.

16 KOPPS
www.kopps-berlin.de

'German vegan' has not been an oxymoron since Kopps opened as Berlin's first high-end, animal-product-free restaurant. The space is sparse but stylish.

17 BERGHAIN/PANORAMA BAR
www.berghain.de

Only world-class DJs heat up this hedonistic labyrinthine ex-power plant pilgrimage club. Hard-edged minimal techno is king at the ex-turbine hall while house dominates at Panorama Bar.

18 ANKERKLAUSE
www.ankerklause.de

Ahoy there! Drop anchor at this nautical kitsch tavern in an old harbour master's shack and enjoy the arse-kicking jukebox, cold beers and surprisingly good German pub fare.

19 LUFTGARTEN
www.luftgarten-berlin.de

On the northern edge of the vast Tempelhofer Feld, a former airport turned public park, this is one of Berlin's loveliest beer gardens. Kick back with a cold brew and a grilled sausage.

20 ZUM STARKEN AUGUST
www.zumstarkenaugust.de

Part circus, part burlesque bar, this vibrant venue dressed in Victorian-era exuberance is a fun addition to the Prenzlauer Berg pub culture, with drag-hosted bingo, burlesque divas and wicked cabaret.

21 BAR JEDER VERNUNFT
www.bar-jeder-vernunft.de

Life's still a cabaret at this intimate 1912 mirrored art-nouveau tent, which puts on sophisticated song-and-dance shows, comedy and chansons nightly.

22 DEUTSCHE OPER BERLIN
www.deutscheoperberlin.de

The German Opera was founded by local citizens in 1912 as a counterpoint to the royal opera. It presents a classic 19th-century opera repertory with a focus on Verdi, Puccini, Wager and Strauss.

23 FREILUFTKINO FRIEDRICHSHAIN
www.freiluftkino-berlin.de

This open-air cinema has seating for 1500 on comfortable benches with backrests, plus a lawn with space for 300 more film fans.

24 HEBBEL AM UFER
www.hebbel-am-ufer.de

Germany's most avant-garde and trailblazing theatre comes with a mission to explore the changes in the social and political fabric of society, often by blurring the lines between theatre, dance and art.

25 BEARPIT KARAOKE
www.bearpitkaraoke.com

On most summer Sundays, Berlin's best free entertainment kicks off at around 3pm when Joe Hatchiban sets up his custom-made mobile karaoke unit in the Mauerpark's amphitheatre.

26 MANUFACTUM
www.manufactum.de

Long before sustainable became a buzzword, this shop stocked traditionally made quality products from around the world, many of which have stood the test of time.

27 DUSSMANN – DAS KULTURKAUFHAUS
www.kulturkaufhaus.de

It's easy to lose track of time in this cultural playground with wall-to-wall books leaving no genre unaccounted for, a downstairs cafe and a performance space.

28 RAUSCH SCHOKOLADENHAUS
www.rausch.de

If the Aztecs thought of chocolate as the elixir of the gods, then this emporium of truffles and pralines must be heaven.

29 MARKTHALLE NEUN
www.markthalleneun.de

This delightful 1891 market hall with its iron-beam-supported ceiling is home to local and regional producers. On Street Food Thursday a couple of dozen international chefs serve delicious snacks from around the world.

30 LP12 MALL OF BERLIN
www.mallofberlin.de

This contemporary retail quarter is tailor-made for black-belt mall rats. More than 270 shops vie for your shopping euros.

PRAGUE

START

HRADČANY

STARÉ MĚSTO PRAŽSKÉ

MALÁ STRANA

SMÍCHOV

PODSKALÍ

Prague is the equal of Paris in terms of beauty, with its spectacle of a 14th-century stone bridge, a hilltop castle and the lovely, lazy Vltava river. Its history goes back a millennium. And the beer? Some of the best in Europe. Prague's maze of cobbled lanes and hidden courtyards is a paradise for the aimless wanderer, always beckoning you to explore a little further.

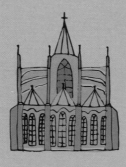

1 PRAGUE CASTLE
www.hrad.cz

Prague Castle is the city's most popular attraction. Looming above the Vltava's left bank, its serried ranks of spires, towers and palaces dominate the city centre like a fairytale fortress.

2 ST VITUS CATHEDRAL
www.katedralasvatehovita.cz

Built over almost 600 years, St Vitus is one of the most richly endowed cathedrals in central Europe, and houses treasures pivotal to the religious and cultural life of the Czech Republic.

6 JOHN LENNON WALL

After his murder on 8 December 1980, John Lennon became a pacifist hero for many young Czechs: his image was painted on a wall in a secluded square opposite the French Embassy.

7 STAROPRAMEN BREWERY
www.staropramen.com

More of a museum visit than an actual brewery tour, the presentation here focuses on the 100-plus years of history of the brewery, the only big Czech brewer based in Prague.

8 MUSEUM OF DECORATIVE ARTS
www.upm.cz

The four halls of this museum are a feast for the eyes, full of 16th- to 19th-century artefacts such as furniture, tapestries, porcelain and a fabulous collection of glasswork.

9 VYŠEHRAD CEMETERY
www.praha-vysehrad.cz

Vyšehrad Cemetery is a main attraction for many visitors, being the final resting place for dozens of Czech luminaries, including Antonín Dvořák, Bedřich Smetana and Alfons Mucha.

10 CHARLES BRIDGE

Strolling across Charles Bridge is everybody's favourite Prague activity. However, by 9am it's a 500m-long fairground, with an army of tourists and hawkers. Experience the bridge at its most atmospheric at dawn, where you can wander more peacefully beneath the impassive gaze of baroque statues.

11 SOPHIE'S HOSTEL
www.sophieshostel.com

This hostel has a touch of contemporary style here, with oak-veneer floors and stark, minimalist decor, along with neutral colours, chunky timber, quirky metal-framed beds and 'designer' showers.

12 NEJEN BISTRO
www.nejenbistro.cz

Nejen (Not Only) has a quirky interior nominated for a slew of design awards, but just as much attention is lavished on the food, which makes the most of the kitchen's fancy Josper grill.

13 LETENSKÝ ZÁMEČEK
www.letenskyzamecek.cz

An upscale brasserie occupying the ground floor of a 19th-century chateau. It's open year-round but its terrace (and Old Town view) comes into its own from May to September.

14 LEEDA
www.leeda.cz

This shop and label, created by two young Prague designers, Lucie Kutálková and Lucie Trnkov, has a well-earned reputation for turning out colourful, hip and stylish clothes – and all at very reasonable prices.

15 NÁPLAVKA FARMERS MARKET
www.farmarsketrziste.cz

This weekly market makes the most of its riverside setting, with live music and outdoor tables scattered among stalls selling bread, vegetables, cakes, wild mushrooms and honey, cider and more.

3 VELETRŽNÍ PALÁC
www.ngprague.cz

The National Gallery's collection of 'Art of the 19th, 20th and 21st Centuries' is a strong contender for Prague's best museum, with a rich collection of world masters.

4 TV TOWER
www.towerpark.cz

Prague's tallest landmark – and depending on your tastes, either its ugliest or its most futuristic feature – is the 216m-tall TV Tower, erected between 1985 and 1992.

5 FUTURA GALLERY
www.futuraproject.cz

The Futura Gallery focuses on all aspects of contemporary art. In the garden, you'll find a rather shocking and amusing permanent installation by David Černý, called 'Brownnosers'.

VIENNA

Baroque streetscapes and imperial palaces set the stage for Vienna's artistic and musical masterpieces, alongside its coffee-house culture and vibrant epicurean and design scenes. With a rich musical heritage, Vienna is known as the City of Music.

JOSEFSTADT

SCHMELZ

LAIMGRUBE

WI

13

MARGARETEN

START

1 HAUS DER MUSIK
www.hausdermusik.com

The Haus der Musik explains the world of sound and music in an amusing and interactive way. Exhibits cover everything from Vienna's Philharmonic Orchestra to street noises.

2 STEPHANSDOM
www.stephanskirche.at

A Gothic masterpiece, cathedral Stephansdom is Vienna's pride and joy. The first thing you'll notice is the glorious tiled roof; inside the church, a magnificent Gothic stone pulpit presides over the main nave.

3 CHRISTKINDLMÄRKTE
www.wien.info/en/shopping-wining-dining/markets/christmas-markets

Vienna's much-loved Christmas market season runs from around mid-November to Christmas Eve. Magical Christkindlmärkte is set up in streets and squares, with stalls selling wooden toys, holiday decorations and traditional food.

6 SPANISH RIDING SCHOOL
www.srs.at

The world-famous Spanish Riding School is a Viennese institution truly reminiscent of the imperial Habsburg era. The unequalled equestrian show is performed by Lipizzaner stallions.

7 SIGMUND FREUD MUSEUM
www.freud-museum.at

This is where Sigmund Freud spent his most prolific years and developed the most significant of his groundbreaking theories; he moved here with his family in 1891 and stayed until 1938.

8 J&L LOBMEYR VIENNA
www.lobmeyr.at

This is one of Vienna's most lavish retail experiences. The collection of Biedermeier pieces, Loos-designed sets, fine or arty glassware and porcelain on display glitters in the light of the chandelier-festooned atrium.

9 WALD & WIESE
www.waldundwiese.at

Some 5000 bee colonies and 600 beekeepers harvest honey within Vienna's city limits. The fruits of their labour are sold at this specialist honey boutique.

10 SCHLOSS SCHÖNBRUNN

The Habsburgs' overwhelmingly opulent summer palace is now a Unesco World Heritage site. Of the palace's 1441 rooms, 40 are open to the public.

11 GRIECHENBEISL
www.griechenbeisl.at

Dating from 1447 and frequented by Beethoven, Brahms, Schubert and Strauss, Vienna's oldest restaurant has vaulted rooms and wood panelling. Every classic Viennese dish is on the menu.

12 PLACHUTTA
www.plachutta.at

If you're keen to taste Tafelspitz, you can't beat this specialist wood-panelled, white-tableclothed restaurant. It serves no fewer than 13 varieties from different cuts of beef.

13 STAATSOPER
www.wiener-staatsoper.at

The glorious Staatsoper is Vienna's premiere opera and classical-music venue. Productions are lavish, formal affairs, where people dress up accordingly.

14 BURGTHEATER
www.burgtheater.at

One of the foremost theatres in the German-speaking world, staging some 800 performances a year, ranging from Shakespeare to Woody Allen.

15 HOTEL SACHER
www.sacher.com

Stepping into Hotel Sacher is like turning back the clocks 100 years. The lobby's dark-wood panelling, original oil paintings, deep red shades and heavy gold chandelier, are reminiscent of a *fin de siècle* bordello.

4 PRATER
www.wiener-prater.at

Spread across 60 sq km (20 sq miles), central Vienna's biggest park comprises woodlands of poplar and chestnut, meadows and tree-lined boulevards, as well as children's playgrounds, a swimming pool, golf course and race track.

5 HOFBURG PALACE
www.hofburg-wien.at

Nothing symbolises Austria's resplendent cultural heritage more than its Hofburg, home base of the Habsburgs from 1273 to 1918. The palace houses the Austrian president's offices and a raft of museums.

STOCKHOLM

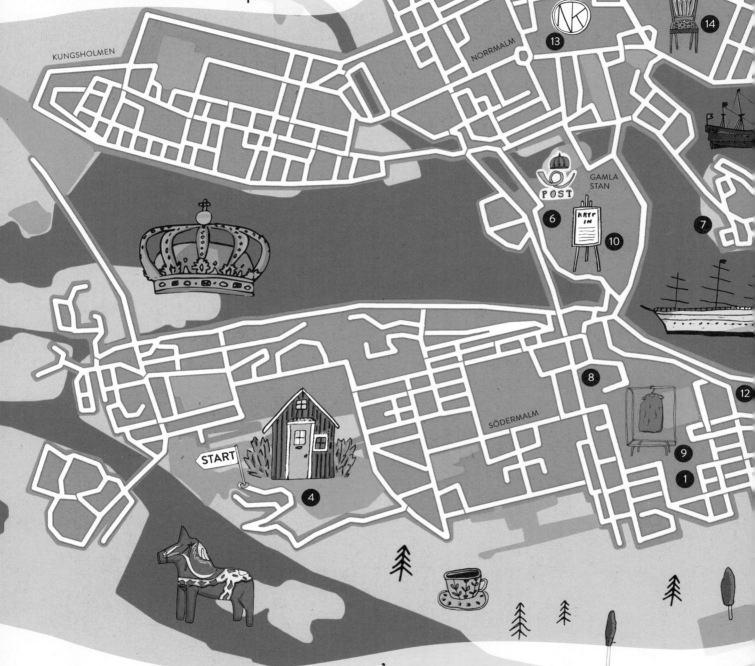

Stockholm's beauty and fashion sense could almost be intimidating. But get to know it better and there is little that is daunting about this top model city. Despite being spread across 14 islands, Stockholm's 57 bridges mean that it is well-connected and compact.

KUNGSHOLMEN

NORRMALM

GAMLA STAN

SÖDERMALM

START

① SOFO

You know you've arrived when a cultural behemoth like *Vogue* magazine declares you the third coolest neighbourhood in the entire world...and the area SoFo in the district of Sodermalm lives up to the hype.

② ÖSTERMALMS SALUHALL MARKET
www.saluhallen.com

Östermalms Saluhall, renovated in 2018, is a must-see for both the architecture and the gourmet food-hall atmosphere. Outdoors it's a many-spired brick confection; indoors it's a sophisticated take on the traditional market, with fresh produce and baked goods, and some of the city's favourite places to grab a meal.

⑤ ABBA: THE MUSEUM
www.abbathemuseum.com

A sensory-overload experience, this long-awaited and wildly hyped cathedral to the demigods of Swedish pop is packed to the gills with memorabilia and interactivity.

⑥ POSTMUSEUM
www.postmuseum.se

Examining almost four centuries of Swedish postal history, the Postmuseum features old mail carriages, kitsch postcards and a cute children's post office.

⑦ VANDRARHEM AF CHAPMAN & SKEPPSHOLMEN
www.stfchapman.com

The af Chapman is a vessel that has done plenty of travelling of its own. It's now anchored in a superb location, swaying gently off Skeppsholmen, and bunks are in hostel dorms below deck.

⑧ KVARNEN

An old-school Hammarby football fan hangout, Kvarnen is one of the best bars in Söder. The gorgeous beer hall dates from 1907 and seeps tradition.

⑨ GRANDPA

Inspired by the hotels of the French Riviera during the '70s, Grandpa's Stockholm location is crammed with atmosphere as well as artfully chosen vintage and faux-vintage clothing.

⑩ KRYP IN
www.restaurangkrypin.nu

Small but perfectly formed, this spot wows diners with creative takes on traditional Swedish dishes. The service is seamless and the atmosphere classy without being stuffy.

⑪ LISA ELMQVIST
www.lisaelmqvist.se

Seafood fans, look no further. This legendary Stockholm restaurant is never short of a satisfied lunchtime crowd, and the menu changes daily, so let the waiters order for you.

⑫ HERMANS TRÄDGÅRDSCAFÉ
www.hermans.se

The justifiably popular vegetarian buffet at this eatery is one of the nicest places to dine in Stockholm, with a glassed-in porch and terrace overlooking the city's glittering skyline.

⑬ NK
www.nk.se

An ultra-classy department store founded in 1902, NK (Nordiska Kompaniet) is a city landmark – you can see its rotating neon sign from most parts of Stockholm.

⑭ SVENSKT TENN
www.sveriskttenn.se

This iconic store is a great way to get a quick handle on what people mean by 'classic Swedish design'.

⑮ SVENSK SLÖJD
www.svenskslojd.se

If you like the traditional Swedish wooden horses, but want one that looks a little unique, check out this shop.

③ VASAMUSEET
www.vasamuseet.se

The home of the massive warship Vasa; it was the pride of the Swedish crown when it started its maiden voyage in 1628, but within minutes it sank to the bottom of Saltsjön.

④ TANTOLUNDEN

Tantolunden is one of Stockholm's most extensive and varied parks. Its combination of allotments, open expanses, outdoor gym, play area and waterside walks make it a great getaway from the city centre.

BUDAPEST

Budapest is an explorer's paradise. Keep your senses primed and you'll discover something wonderful at every turn. The city is a treasure trove of baroque, neoclassical, eclectic and art nouveau buildings and quirky ruin bars. The land is also blessed with an abundance of hot springs.

LIPOTVARO

BALTAZAR

START

8

1

CASTLE HILL

2

9

12

3

6

5

13

INNER CITY

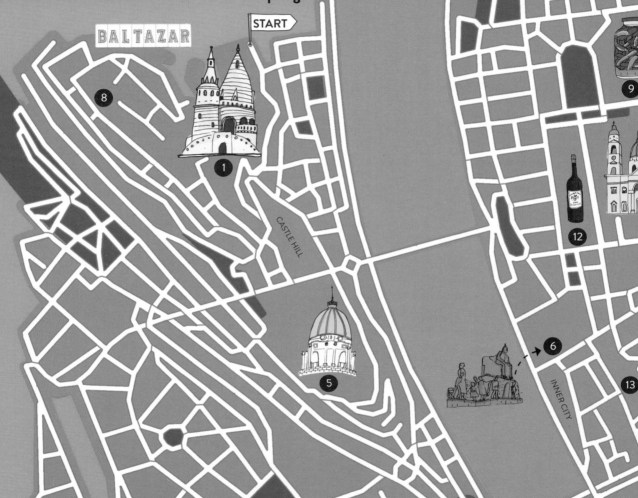

② PARLIAMENT

www.hungarianparliament.com

The Eclectic-style Parliament, completed in 1902, has 691 sumptuously decorated rooms. The Crown of St Stephen, the nation's most important national icon, is on display in the Domed Hall.

① FISHERMEN'S BASTION

This neo-Gothic monument looks medieval and offers some of the best views in Budapest. The seven gleaming white turrets represent the Magyar tribes that entered the Carpathian Basin in the late 9th century.

③ BASILICA OF ST STEPHEN

www.basilica.hu

Budapest's neoclassical cathedral was built over half a century and completed in 1905. The basilica is rather dark and gloomy inside, but take a trip to the top of the dome for incredible views.

6 VÖRÖSMARTY TÉR

In the centre of this large square surrounded by smart shops, galleries and cafes is a statue of Mihály Vörösmarty, the 19th-century poet after whom the square is named.

7 HOTEL RUM

www.hotelrumbudapest.com

The 38 guestrooms at this whimsical design hotel fall into four categories, each named after a different rum. Blonde wood, capsule espresso machines and a cream-and-charcoal colour scheme feature throughout.

8 BALTAZÁR

www.baltazarbudapest.com

This family-run boutique hotel at the northern end of the Castle District has 11 individually decorated rooms decked out with vintage furniture and striking wallpaper.

9 KISPIAC

This hole-in-the-wall retro-style restaurant serves seriously Hungarian things like stuffed *csülök* (pig's trotter – way better than it sounds), roast *malac* (piglet) and an infinite variety of *savanyúság* (pickled vegetables).

10 M RESTAURANT

www.metterem.hu

A small, romantic spot with a laid-back vibe, brown-paper-bag decor and a short – but very well thought-out – menu of Hungarian dishes with a French twist.

11 BARACK & SZILVA

www.barackesszilva.hu

This is the kind of perfectly formed restaurant that every neighbourhood wishes it could boast. 'Peach & Pear' serves high-quality, exceptionally well-prepared Hungarian provincial food in a bistro setting.

12 MALATINSZKY WINE STORE

www.malatinszky.hu

Owned and operated by a one-time sommelier at the Gundel restaurant, this shop has an excellent selection of high-end Hungarian wines, including three vintages from his own organically farmed vines.

13 BOMO ART

www.bomoart.hu

This tiny shop just off Váci utca sells some of the finest paper and paper goods in Budapest, including leather-bound notebooks, photo albums and address books.

14 SZIMPLA KERT

Budapest's first *romkocsmá* (ruin pub), Szimpla Kert is firmly on the drinking-tourists' trail. It's a huge complex with nooks filled with bric-a-brac, graffiti, art and all manner of unexpected items.

15 HEREND

www.herend.com

For both contemporary and traditional fine porcelain, there is no other shop to go but Herend. Among the more popular motifs is the Victoria pattern of butterflies and wildflowers.

4 HOUSE OF TERROR

www.terrorhaza.hu

The headquarters of the dreaded secret police is now the startling House of Terror, a museum focusing on the crimes and atrocities of Hungary's fascist and Stalinist regimes in a permanent exhibition called Double Occupation.

5 ROYAL PALACE

The former Royal Palace has been razed and rebuilt at least half a dozen times over the past seven centuries. Today, it contains the Hungarian National Gallery, the Castle Museum and the National Széchenyi Library.

KRAKÓW

N
NE
E
SE
S
SW
W
NW

PIASEK

START

STARE MIASTO

KAZIMIERZ

11

3

10

14

15

6

5

13

8

7

1

4

9

12

A mythical atmosphere – perhaps stemming from the famous Wawel dragon legend – permeates attractive streets and squares. As you walk through Kraków's Old Town, you'll sometimes find yourself overwhelmed by the harmony of a quiet back street, the 'just so' nature of the architecture and light.

① WAWEL CATHEDRAL
www.katedra-wawelska.pl

The Royal Cathedral has witnessed many coronations, funerals and burials of Poland's monarchs and strongmen over the centuries. This is the third church on this site, consecrated in 1364.

② SCHINDLER'S FACTORY
www.mhk.pl/branches/oskar-schindlers-factory

This impressive interactive museum is housed in the former enamel factory of Oskar Schindler, the Nazi industrialist who famously saved the lives of members of his Jewish labour force during the Holocaust.

⑤ COLLEGIUM MAIUS

www.maius.uj.edu.pl

The Collegium Maius, built as part of the Kraków Academy, is the oldest surviving university building in Poland, and a shining example of 15th-century Gothic architecture in the city.

⑥ RYNEK UNDERGROUND

www.podziemiarynku.com

This fascinating attraction beneath the market square consists of an underground route through medieval market stalls and other long-forgotten chambers.

⑦ MUNDO HOSTEL

www.mundohostel.eu

Well-maintained hostel in a quiet courtyard. Each room is themed as a different country.

⑧ WIELOPOLE

www.wielopole.pl

Hotel Wielopole's selection of bright, modern rooms is housed in a renovated block with a great courtyard.

⑨ METROPOLITAN BOUTIQUE HOTEL

www.hotelmetropolitan.pl

An excellent choice for travellers who seek comfort in a Kazimierz location, this luxury boutique fuses modern design within the confines of a 19th-century townhouse.

⑩ ED RED

www.edred.pl

This restaurant is a solid splurge option for the steaks, made from dry-aged beef and using only local producers.

⑪ GLONOJAD

www.glonojad.com

Attractive and much-lauded, this vegetarian restaurant has a great view onto Plac Matejki. The diverse menu has a variety of tasty dishes plus an all-day breakfast menu.

⑫ BŁAŻKO JEWELLERY

www.blazko.pl

The eye-catching creations of designer Grzegorz Błażko are on display in this gallery and workshop, including his unique range of chequered enamel jewellery.

⑬ GALERIA PLAKATU

www.cracowpostergallery.com

Poland has always excelled in the art of making film posters, and this shop has the city's largest and best choice.

⑭ BORUNI AMBER MUSEUM

www.ambermuseum.eu

One-stop shopping for amberphiles. Cases upon cases of amber rings, necklaces, brooches and earrings, plus a 'museum' at the back.

③ MUSEUM OF PHARMACY

www.muzeumfarmacji.pl

Accommodated in a beautiful historic townhouse worth the visit alone, the museum features a 22,000-piece collection, which includes laboratory equipment, pharmaceutical instruments and glassware.

④ WAWEL CASTLE

www.wawel.krakow.pl

As the political and cultural heart of Poland through the 16th and 17th centuries, Wawel Castle is a potent symbol of national identity. Now a museum, the State Rooms and Royal Private Apartments are most impressive.

⑮ CLOTH HALL

www.mnk.pl

Once the centre of Kraków's medieval clothing trade, now a busy centre for crafts and souvenirs; the upper floor houses the Sukiennice (Gallery of 19th-Century Polish Painting).

ATHENS

With equal measures of grunge and grace, Athens is a heady mix of history and edginess. Cultural and social life plays out amid, around and in ancient landmarks. The magnificent Acropolis, visible from almost every part of the city, reminds Greeks daily of their heritage and the city's many transformations.

EXARHIA

PSYRI

THISIO

PLAKA

KOUKAKI

10

13

4

14

9

1

2

6

7

8

3

FINISH

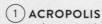

(1) ACROPOLIS

www.odysseus.culture.gr

The Acropolis is one of the most important ancient sites in the Western world. Crowned by the Parthenon, it stands sentinel over Athens.

(2) DIONYSOS

www.dionysoszonars.gr

Directly across from the Acropolis main entrance, this restaurant is ground zero for tour-bus lunches. But you could do a lot worse if you're in need of a restorative coffee.

(3) NATIONAL MUSEUM OF CONTEMPORARY ART

www.emst.gr

In its spectacularly renovated quarters at the former Fix Brewery on Leoforos Syngrou, this museum shows top-notch exhibitions of Greek and international contemporary art, including installations, video and new media, and experimental architecture.

START ▷

KOLONAKI

⑥ ILIAS LALAOUNIS JEWELLERY MUSEUM

Jewellery and decorative arts inspired by various periods in Greek history showcase the talents of Greece's renowned jeweller Ilias Lalaounis.

⑦ ATHENS BACKPACKERS
www.facebook.com/athensstudios

The rooftop bar with cheap drinks and Acropolis views is a major drawcard for this modern and friendly backpacker hostel favourite.

⑧ HERA HOTEL
www.herahotel.gr

This elegant boutique hotel was totally rebuilt – but the formal interior design is in keeping with the lovely neoclassical façade. Spectacular views.

⑨ ELECTRA PALACE
www.electrahotels.gr

Plaka's smartest hotel is one for the romantics – have breakfast under the Acropolis on your balcony and dinner in the chic rooftop restaurant.

⑩ VARVAKIOS AGORA

The streets around the colourful and bustling Varvakios Agora are a sensory delight. The meat and fish market fills the historic building on the eastern side, and the fruit and vegetable market is across the road.

⑪ YIANTES

This modern eatery, with its white linen and fresh-cut flowers set in a lovely garden courtyard, is upmarket for Exarhia, but the food is superb and made with largely organic produce.

⑫ SPONDI
www.spondi.gr

Two Michelin-starred Spondi is frequently voted Athens' best restaurant. It offers Mediterranean haute cuisine, with heavy French influences, in a relaxed, chic setting in a charming old house.

⑬ MONASTIRAKI FLEA MARKET

This traditional market has a festive atmosphere. Permanent antique and collectables shops are open all week, while the streets around the station and Adrianou fill with vendors selling jewellery, handicrafts and bric-a-brac.

④ ANCIENT AGORA
www.odysseus.culture.gr

This was the heart of ancient Athens, the lively focal point of administrative, commercial, political and social activity. Socrates expounded his philosophy here, and St Paul came here to win converts to Christianity.

⑭ FORGET ME NOT
www.forgetmenotathens.gr

This impeccable small store stocks super-cool design gear, from fashion to housewares and gifts, all by contemporary Greek designers, from cheerful 'evil eye' coasters to Herme's rubber beach sandals.

⑤ NATIONAL GARDENS

A delightful, shady refuge during summer, the National Gardens were formerly the royal gardens, designed by Queen Amalia. There's a large children's playground, a duck pond and a shady cafe.

⑮ KOLONAKI FARMERS MARKET

Every week, Kolonaki welcomes the shopping bustle of a *laiki* (farmers market). The local regulars come to buy fresh fruit, vegetables, fish, olives, honey, handmade products and flowers.

ST PETERSBURG

START

VASILEOSTROVSKY DISTRICT

PETROGRADSKY DISTRICT

Russia's imperial capital's history and grandeur never fails to amaze. Whether cruising the elegant canals or crossing one of the 342 bridges, you're never far from water. The city is a treasure trove of art and culture, with world-class museums, palaces, art galleries, ballet, opera and classical concerts. Summer White Nights are legendary here, when the sun barely dips below the horizon, but it's just as beautiful in winter covered in snow.

① CHURCH OF THE SAVIOUR ON THE SPILLED BLOOD
www.cathedral.ru

This five-domed dazzler is the city's most elaborate church, with a Russian Orthodox exterior, and an interior decorated with some 7000 sq metres of mosaics.

② PETER & PAUL FORTRESS
www.spbmuseum.ru

Housing a cathedral where the Romanovs are buried, a former prison and various exhibitions, this large defensive fortress on Zayachy Island is the kernel from which St Petersburg grew into the city it is today.

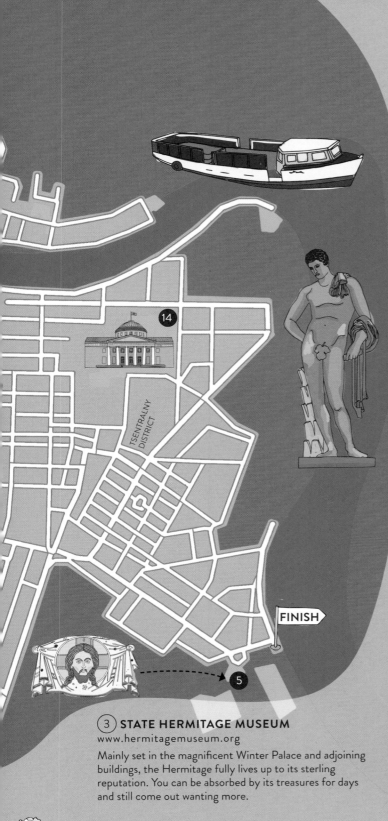

6 ERARTA MUSEUM OF CONTEMPORARY ART
www.erarta.com

This fantastic contemporary art museum has made this far-flung area of Vasilyevsky Island a destination in itself. The museum divides neatly into two parts, spread over five floors.

7 SOUL KITCHEN HOSTEL
www.soulkitchenhostel.com

Soul Kitchen blends boho hipness and boutique-hotel comfort, scoring perfect 10s in many key categories: private rooms, dorm beds, common areas, kitchen and bathrooms.

8 DOSTOEVSKY MUSEUM
www.md.spb.ru

Fyodor Dostoevsky lived in flats all over the city, but his final residence is this 'memorial flat', where he lived from 1878 until he died in 1881. The apartment remains as it was when the Dostoevsky family lived here, including the study where he wrote *The Brothers Karamazov*.

9 RACHMANINOV ANTIQUE HOTEL
www.hotelrachmaninov.com

The long-established Rachmaninov still feels like a secret place for those in the know. It's pleasantly old world with hardwood floors and attractive Russian furnishings.

10 ROSSI HOTEL
www.rossihotels.com

Occupying a beautifully restored building on a pretty square, the Rossi's 53 rooms are all designed differently, but their brightness and moulded ceilings are uniform.

11 UDELNAYA FAIR

This market is a treasure trove of Soviet ephemera, pre-revolutionary antiques, WWII artefacts and bonkers kitsch from all eras; truly worth travelling for.

12 NORTHWAY

There is quite simply no bigger collection of *matryoshki* (nesting dolls), amber, fur and other souvenir staples than that on offer at this impressive and stylish shop on the Neva embankment.

13 FINLAND STATION

Rebuilt in the 1970s in rectilinear Soviet style, the *Finlyandsky vokzal* endures as a place of historical significance, where Lenin finally arrived in 1917 after 17 years in exile abroad.

14 TAURIDE PALACE

Catherine the Great had this baroque palace built in 1783 for Grigory Potemkin, a famed general and her companion for many years of her life. Once the romping grounds of the tsarina, the gardens are now open to all, and their facilities include a lake, several cafes and an entertainment centre.

15 THE BROTHERS KARAMAZOV

Pack a copy of Dostoevsky's final novel to read while staying at this appealing boutique hotel – the great man penned *The Brothers Karamazov* while living in the neighbourhood. In homage, the hotel's 28 charming rooms are all named after different female Dostoevsky characters.

3 STATE HERMITAGE MUSEUM
www.hermitagemuseum.org

Mainly set in the magnificent Winter Palace and adjoining buildings, the Hermitage fully lives up to its sterling reputation. You can be absorbed by its treasures for days and still come out wanting more.

4 MARIINSKY THEATRE
www.mariinsky.ru

The Mariinsky Theatre has played a pivotal role in Russian ballet ever since it was built in 1859, and remains one of Russia's most loved and respected cultural institutions.

5 ALEXANDER NEVSKY MONASTERY
www.lavra.spb.ru

The Alexander Nevsky Monastery – named for the patron saint of St Petersburg – is the city's most ancient and eminent monastery. In 1797 it became a lavra, the most senior grade of Russian Orthodox monasteries.

MARRAKESH

Marrakesh's sights and sounds will dazzle and enchant. This vibrant city exists at the edge of the Sahara, hemmed in by High Atlas passes. Religion permeates the rhythms of daily life; hear the call to prayer echo out from the mosques. The medina is ideal to explore private palaces and mansions, and the souqs are a magpie's nest of treasures.

RIAD LAAROUS

BAB DOUKKALA

RMILA

MOUASSINE

KENNARIA

① LE TOBSIL
In this intimate *riad* (traditional Moroccan house) restaurant, 50 guests (maximum) indulge in five-course Moroccan menus with aperitifs and wine pairings, as *Gnaoua* musicians strum quietly in the courtyard.

② KOUTOUBIA MOSQUE
Five times a day, one voice rises above the Djemaa din as the *muezzin* calls the faithful to prayer from the Koutoubia Mosque minaret.

③ KASBAH MOSQUE
Built in 1190, the Kasbah Mosque is the main mosque for the southern end of the medina. If you were wondering what Marrakesh's famed Koutoubia Minaret would have looked like when it was covered in pink plaster, the mosque's pastel-pink minaret gives you a fair idea.

FINISH

10

⑥ ALI BEN YOUSSEF MEDERSA

Entry to this Quranic learning centre will display carved cedar cupolas and *mashrabiyya* (wooden-lattice screen) balconies, while the courtyard is a mind-boggling profusion of Hispano-Moresque ornament: five-colour walls, stucco archways and a marble mihrab.

⑦ DJEMAA EL-FNA

Everywhere you look in Marrakesh's main square, you'll discover drama in progress. Hoopla and *halqa* (street theatre) has been non-stop here since 1050.

⑧ MUSÉE DE MARRAKESH

www.museedemarrakech.ma

The museum exhibits a collection of Moroccan art forms within the decadent salons of the Mnebhi Palace. The central internal courtyard is the highlight, though don't miss the display of exquisite Fez ceramics.

⑨ BAHIA PALACE

Imagine what you could build with Morocco's top artisans at your service for 14 years: across the complex you'll find intricate marquetry, *zouak* (painted wood) ceilings, original woven-silk panels and stained-glass windows.

⑩ BAB DEBBAGH TANNERIES

The acrid smell assaulting your nose announces your arrival in the tannery area in the central souqs. Come in the morning to see tanners at work, transforming leather hides into a rainbow of hues.

⑪ SOUQ DES TEINTURIERS

The dyers' souq is one of Marrakesh's most colourful market sights. Here you'll find skeins of coloured wool draped from the rafters and a rainbow of pigment pots.

⑫ HOTEL LE GALLIA

www.hotellegallia.com

Le Gallia maintains comfortable, neat-as-a-pin rooms, arranged around a courtyard trimmed with colourful *beldi* tiles and shaded by orange trees.

⑬ RIAD AZOULAY

www.riad-azoulay.com

The restoration of this 300-year-old mansion hotel has resulted in a haven of casual luxury where original cedar ceilings and plasterwork decor sit comfortably alongside modern art, painted-wood antique furniture and sumptuously coloured *kilims*.

⑭ COOPERATIVE ARTISANALE DES FEMMES DE MARRAKESH

A showcase for Marrakesh's female *mâalems* (master artisans), the cooperative is eye-opening and a total bargain. Find original, handcrafted designs or ask about getting tunics and dresses tailor-made.

⑮ APOTHICAIRE TUAREG

Serious foodies, you have found spice nirvana. This old-fashioned shop is crammed to the rafters with both day-to-day cooking spices and the more unusual natural remedies that Moroccans use to cure illnesses.

④ DAR MOHA

www.darmoha.ma

Restaurant Dar Moha's Mohamed Fedal is Morocco's foremost celebrity chef, giving taste buds a treat with updated local classics. The evening *diffa* (feast) is a five-course extravaganza that highlights the Moroccan sweet-savoury obsession.

⑤ MUSÉE BOUCHAROUITE

Berber boucharouites may be a poor cousin to the famous jewel-toned Moroccan carpets, but this beautifully collated gallery housed in an 18th-century riad displays the artistry of this lesser-known craft.

CAPE TOWN

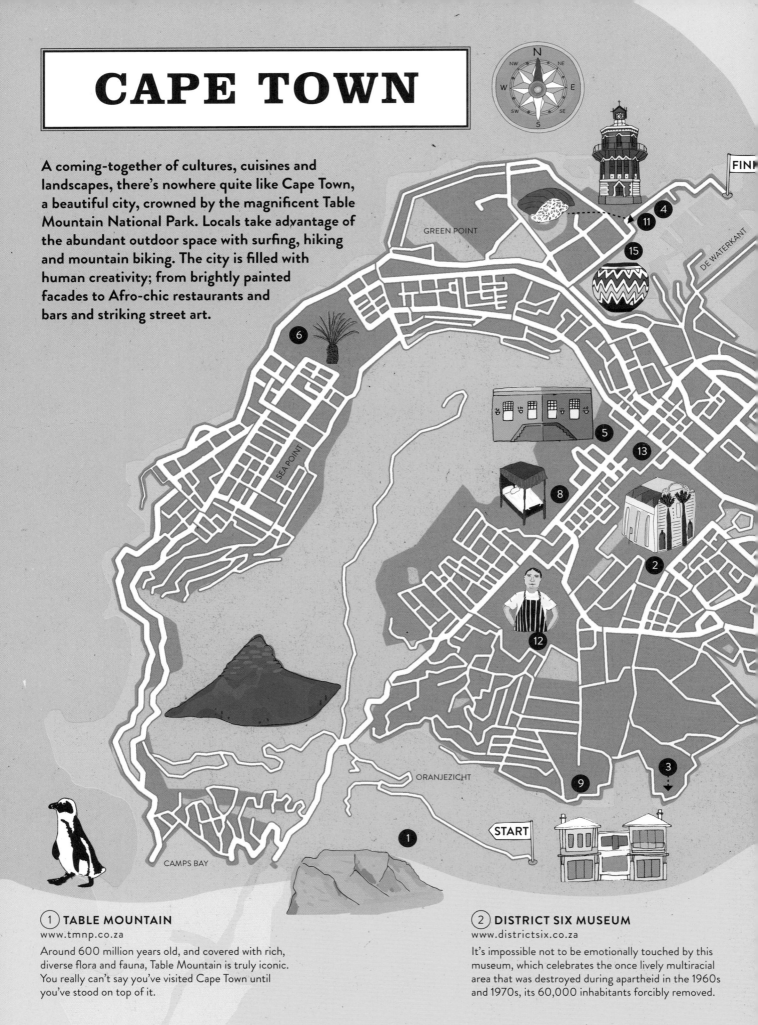

A coming-together of cultures, cuisines and landscapes, there's nowhere quite like Cape Town, a beautiful city, crowned by the magnificent Table Mountain National Park. Locals take advantage of the abundant outdoor space with surfing, hiking and mountain biking. The city is filled with human creativity; from brightly painted facades to Afro-chic restaurants and bars and striking street art.

GREEN POINT

DE WATERKANT

FINI

SEA POINT

ORANJEZICHT

START

CAMPS BAY

(1) TABLE MOUNTAIN
www.tmnp.co.za

Around 600 million years old, and covered with rich, diverse flora and fauna, Table Mountain is truly iconic. You really can't say you've visited Cape Town until you've stood on top of it.

(2) DISTRICT SIX MUSEUM
www.districtsix.co.za

It's impossible not to be emotionally touched by this museum, which celebrates the once lively multiracial area that was destroyed during apartheid in the 1960s and 1970s, its 60,000 inhabitants forcibly removed.

③ KIRSTENBOSCH BOTANICAL GARDENS
www.sanbi.org/gardens/kirstenbosch

Location and unique flora make these 52,800-sq-km (20,000-sq-mile) botanical gardens among the world's most beautiful. At the Newlands end, you'll find the information centre, an excellent souvenir shop and the conservatory.

④ V&A WATERFRONT
www.waterfront.co.za

The Alfred and Victoria Basins date from 1860, and this historic working harbour has a spectacular setting and many tourist-oriented attractions, including masses of shops, restaurants, bars, cinemas and cruises.

WOODSTOCK

OBSERVATORY

⑤ BO-KAAP
The Bo-Kaap area, with its vividly painted low-roofed houses – many of them historic monuments – strung along narrow cobbled streets, is one of the most photographed sections of the city.

⑥ SEA POINT PROMENADE
Ambulating along Sea Point's wide, paved and grassy promenade is a pleasure shared by Capetonians from all walks of life – it's a great place to observe the city's multiculturalism.

⑦ WISH U WERE HERE
www.wishuwereherecapetown.com

The designers clearly had a lot of fun with this hotel. One dorm is Barbie-doll pink; another has a suspended fishing boat as a bed; another is styled after an intensive care unit!

⑧ DUTCH MANOR
www.dutchmanor.co.za

Four-poster beds, giant armoires and creaking floorboards lend terrific atmosphere to this six-room hotel crafted from an 1812 building. Dinners can be prepared on request and staff can also arrange Bo-Kaap walking tours.

⑨ MANNABAY
www.mannabay.com

Nothing seems too much bother for the staff at this knockout hotel decorated with stunning pieces of contemporary local art. Its hillside location on the edge of the national park provides amazing views.

⑩ CLIFFORD & SANDRA'S
At the market next to Khayelitsha Station, ask around to find this shack cafe serving some of the tastiest – and certainly the best-value – traditional chow in Cape Town.

⑪ WILLOUGHBY & CO
www.willoughbyandco.co.za

Commonly acknowledged as one of the better places to eat at the Waterfront – and with long queues to prove it. Huge servings of sushi are the standout from a fish-based menu.

⑫ CHEF'S TABLE, BELMOND
www.belmond.com/mountnelsonhotel

There are several dining options at the Mount Nelson Hotel, but for a real treat, book a table with a front-row view onto the drama and culinary magic unfolding inside the kitchen.

⑬ LUVEY 'N ROSE
www.luveynrose.co.za

This smashing gallery mashes up collectable antiques and works by key South African and African artists, such as Walter Battiss, with more contemporary pieces from emerging talents.

⑭ NEIGHBOURGOODS MARKET
www.neighbourgoodsmarket.co.za

The first, and best, of the artisan goods markets now common across the Cape. Food and drinks are gathered in the main area, while the Designergoods area hosts local fashions and accessories.

⑮ WATERSHED
www.waterfront.co.za/shop/watershed

The best place to shop for souvenirs in Cape Town, this exciting revamped retail market gathers together hundreds of top Capetonian and South African brands in fashion, arts, crafts and design.

DUBAI

FINISH

Dubai is a stirring alchemy of profound traditions and ambitious futuristic vision. With Emiratis making up only a fraction of the population, Dubai is a bustling microcosm shared by cultures from all corners of the world. This is a superlative-craving society that has birthed the world's tallest building, an island shaped like a palm tree, a huge indoor ski paradise and the world's fastest rollercoaster.

AL MANKHOOL

AL KARAMA

④

AL BADA'A

①

⑮

③

JUMEIRAH 1

②

DOWNTOWN

JUMEIRAH 2

AL WASL

⑬

⑩

⑦

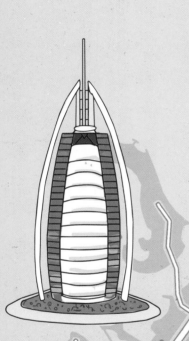

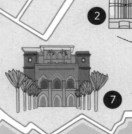

⑪

⑭

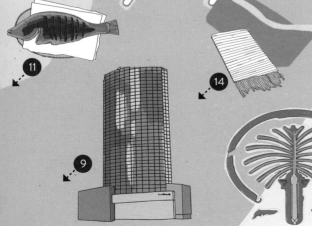

⑨

⑤

⑥

⑩

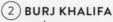

① ETIHAD MUSEUM
www.etihadmuseum.dubaiculture.ae

This museum uses displays, photographs, artefacts and personal accounts to tell the story of the 1971 formation of the UAE, spurred by the discovery of oil and the British withdrawal.

② BURJ KHALIFA
www.atthetop.ae

The Burj Khalifa is the world's tallest building and a stunning feat of architecture and engineering, with two observation decks on the 124th and 148th floors, and a restaurant-bar on the 122nd.

6 CAMEL MUSEUM

This exhibit explains how and why camels are held in such high regard in Arabian culture, and depicts their historical importance and prominence in Arabic literature.

7 PALACE DOWNTOWN DUBAI

www.theaddress.com

Explorers with a romantic streak will be enchanted by this low-lying, luxe lakefront hotel with its winning alchemy of old-world class and Arabic aesthetics.

8 XVA HOTEL

www.xvahotel.com

This art-infused hotel occupies a century-old wind-tower house smack dab in the Al Fahidi Historic District, with 13 compact rooms that open onto a courtyard.

9 MEDIA ONE HOTEL

www.mediaonehotel.com

Match your mood to the room: Hip, Cool, Calm or Chill-Out. This lifestyle hotel loads up on all the Zeitgeist essentials global nomads crave: iPhones, iPod docking stations and satellite TV.

10 MILAS

www.milas.cc

This restaurant, named after a traditional guest-reception room, has a sleek contemporary look – wood, glass, neon – that goes well with updated riffs on traditional local dishes.

11 BU QTAIR

Always packed to the gills, this simple seaside restaurant is a Dubai institution, famous for serving the freshest fish, marinated in a fragrant masala (curry) sauce and cooked to order.

12 AL TAWASOL

At this gem of a restaurant, the best seats are on the carpeted floor of your private Bedouin-style tent with a thin sheet of plastic serving as a 'table cloth'. It's famous for its chicken *mandi* (rice topped with spicy stew).

13 DUBAI MALL

www.thedubaimall.com

With around 1200 stores, this isn't merely the world's largest shopping mall: it's a small city, with a giant ice rink and aquarium, a dinosaur skeleton, indoor theme parks and 150 food outlets.

14 MARINA MARKET

www.marinamarket.ae

This lively market behind the Dubai Marina Mall delivers clothing, handicrafts, jewellery and unusual gift items galore, including upcycled handbags.

15 DUBAI FLEA MARKET

www.dubai-fleamarket.com

Flea markets are like urban archaeology: you'll need patience and luck, but oh, the thrill when finally unearthing a piece of treasure! Trade malls for stalls and look for Dubai bargains.

3 JUMEIRAH MOSQUE

www.cultures.ae

Snowy white and intricately detailed, Jumeirah is Dubai's most beautiful mosque and one of only a handful open to non-Muslims in the UAE, on tours by the Sheikh Mohammed Centre for Cultural Understanding.

4 AL FAHIDI HISTORIC DISTRICT

The labyrinthine lanes of this nicely restored heritage area are flanked by sand-coloured houses topped with wind towers. Explore about 50 buildings containing museums, craft shops and courtyard cafes.

5 GOLD SOUQ

All that glitters is gold (and occasionally silver) at this colourful covered arcade where hundreds of stores overflow with every kind of jewellery imaginable. Best in the evening.

DELHI

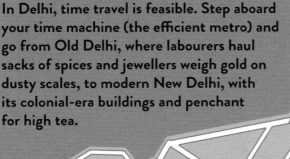

In Delhi, time travel is feasible. Step aboard your time machine (the efficient metro) and go from Old Delhi, where labourers haul sacks of spices and jewellers weigh gold on dusty scales, to modern New Delhi, with its colonial-era buildings and penchant for high tea.

KAROL BAGH

8

12

MEENA BAZAAR

CONNAUGHT PLACE

3

6

15

START

9

DELHI RIDGE

NEW DELHI

4

10 ←

2

11 ↓

② NEHRU PLANETARIUM

www.nehruplanetarium.org

One of the five Nehru planetariums across India established to educate about the solar system; there are shows in English and Hindi.

① AKSHARDHAM

www.akshardham.com

Gandhinagar's only real tourist attraction is this spectacular temple, belonging to the wealthy Hindu Swaminarayan group. Ornately carved and built by nearly 1000 artisans, it's constructed of 6000 tonnes of pink sandstone and surrounded by manicured gardens, and promises to reveal the secret of life after death.

③ JHANDEWALAN HANUMAN TEMPLE

This temple is not to be missed (it's actually hard to miss) if you're in Karol Bagh. Take a short detour to see the 34m-high Hanuman statue that soars above the train tracks.

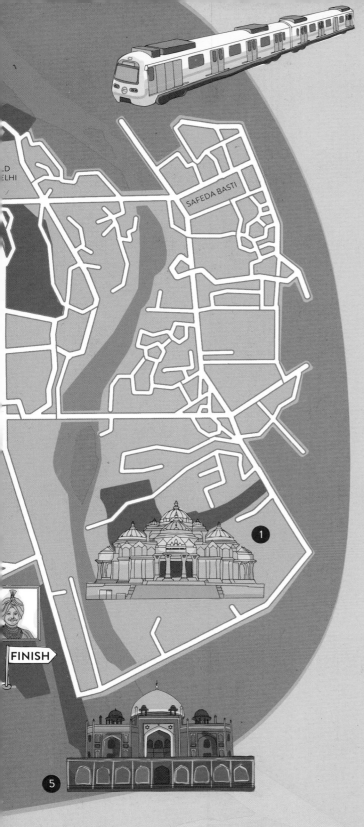

6 QUTB MINAR COMPLEX

If you only have time to visit just one of Delhi's ancient ruins, make it this. The first monuments here were erected by the sultans of Mehrauli, and subsequent rulers set in stone the triumph of Muslim rule.

7 HAZRAT NIZAM-UD-DIN DARGAH

Delhi's most mystical experience is visiting the marble shrine of Muslim Sufi saint Nizam-uddin Auliya. The dargah is hidden in a tangle of bazaars and on Thursday evenings you'll hear Sufis singing Islamic devotional songs.

8 CHANDNI CHOWK

Old Delhi's main drag is lined by Jain, Hindu and Sikh temples, plus a church. Elegant in Mughal times, the thoroughfare is now mind-bendingly chaotic, with tiny little ancient bazaars tentacling off it.

9 MUGHAL GARDENS

The extravagance of these glorious gardens is such that Mountbatten, India's last viceroy, was said to have employed 418 gardeners. There are fountains, cypress, bougainvillea, climbing roses, symmetrical lawns and wandering peacocks.

10 SULABH INTERNATIONAL MUSEUM OF TOILETS

www.sulabhtoiletmuseum.org

Since 1970, the Sulabh NGO has worked to address India's sanitation issues, constructing public toilets and developing pour-flush toilets. Their small, quirky museum traces the water closet's history from 2500 BC to modern times.

11 MADPACKERS HOSTEL

A friendly, relaxed hostel with a bright and airy sitting room that's one of the best places in town to hang out, meet like-minded travellers and maybe even join in with yoga classes.

12 BLOOMROOMS @ NEW DELHI

www.staybloom.com

Bloom Rooms' white-and-yellow, pared-down designer aesthetic is unlike any other hotel in the 'hood, plus there are soft pillows, comfortable beds, good wi-fi and free mineral water.

13 DEVNA

www.tensundernagar.com

Devna is a bed and breakfast with lots of charm, with antique wooden furniture, photographs of maharajas, and works of art. The upstairs rooms open onto small terraces, with views over the pretty courtyard garden.

14 GALI PARANTHE WALI

This lane has been serving up delectable *parathas* (traditional flat bread) fresh off the *tawa* (hotplate) for generations, originally serving pilgrims at the time of the Mughals.

15 RAJDHANI

Thalis (food platters) fit for a king. Treat yourself at this restaurant with food-of-the-gods vegetarian thalis that encompass a fantastic array of Gujarati and Rajasthani dishes.

4 INDIA GATE

This imposing 42m-high stone memorial arch was designed by Edwin Lutyens in 1921. It pays tribute to 90,000 Indian army soldiers who died in WWI, the Northwest Frontier operations and the 1919 Anglo-Afghan War.

5 HUMAYUN'S TOMB

Humayun's tomb is sublimely well proportioned, seeming to float above its symmetrical gardens. Constructed for the Mughal emperor in the mid-16th century by Haji Begum, Humayun's Persian-born wife, it marries Persian and Mughal elements.

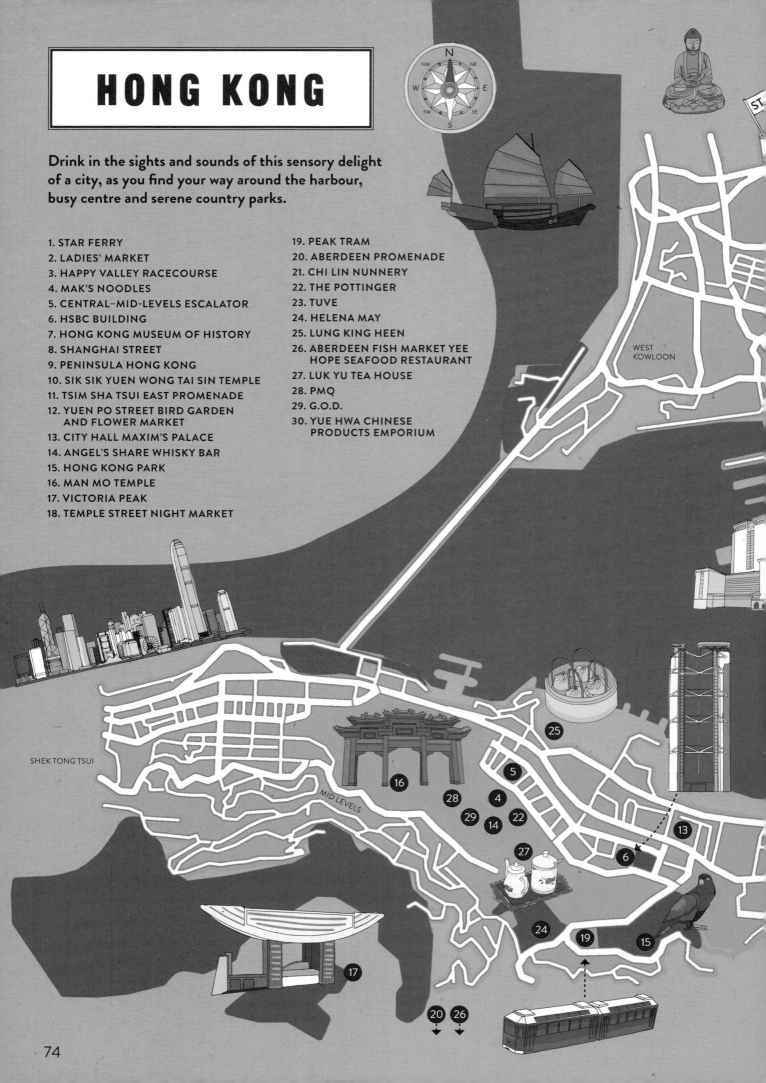

HONG KONG

Drink in the sights and sounds of this sensory delight of a city, as you find your way around the harbour, busy centre and serene country parks.

1. STAR FERRY
2. LADIES' MARKET
3. HAPPY VALLEY RACECOURSE
4. MAK'S NOODLES
5. CENTRAL–MID-LEVELS ESCALATOR
6. HSBC BUILDING
7. HONG KONG MUSEUM OF HISTORY
8. SHANGHAI STREET
9. PENINSULA HONG KONG
10. SIK SIK YUEN WONG TAI SIN TEMPLE
11. TSIM SHA TSUI EAST PROMENADE
12. YUEN PO STREET BIRD GARDEN AND FLOWER MARKET
13. CITY HALL MAXIM'S PALACE
14. ANGEL'S SHARE WHISKY BAR
15. HONG KONG PARK
16. MAN MO TEMPLE
17. VICTORIA PEAK
18. TEMPLE STREET NIGHT MARKET
19. PEAK TRAM
20. ABERDEEN PROMENADE
21. CHI LIN NUNNERY
22. THE POTTINGER
23. TUVE
24. HELENA MAY
25. LUNG KING HEEN
26. ABERDEEN FISH MARKET YEE HOPE SEAFOOD RESTAURANT
27. LUK YU TEA HOUSE
28. PMQ
29. G.O.D.
30. YUE HWA CHINESE PRODUCTS EMPORIUM

WEST KOWLOON

SHEK TONG TSUI

MID LEVELS

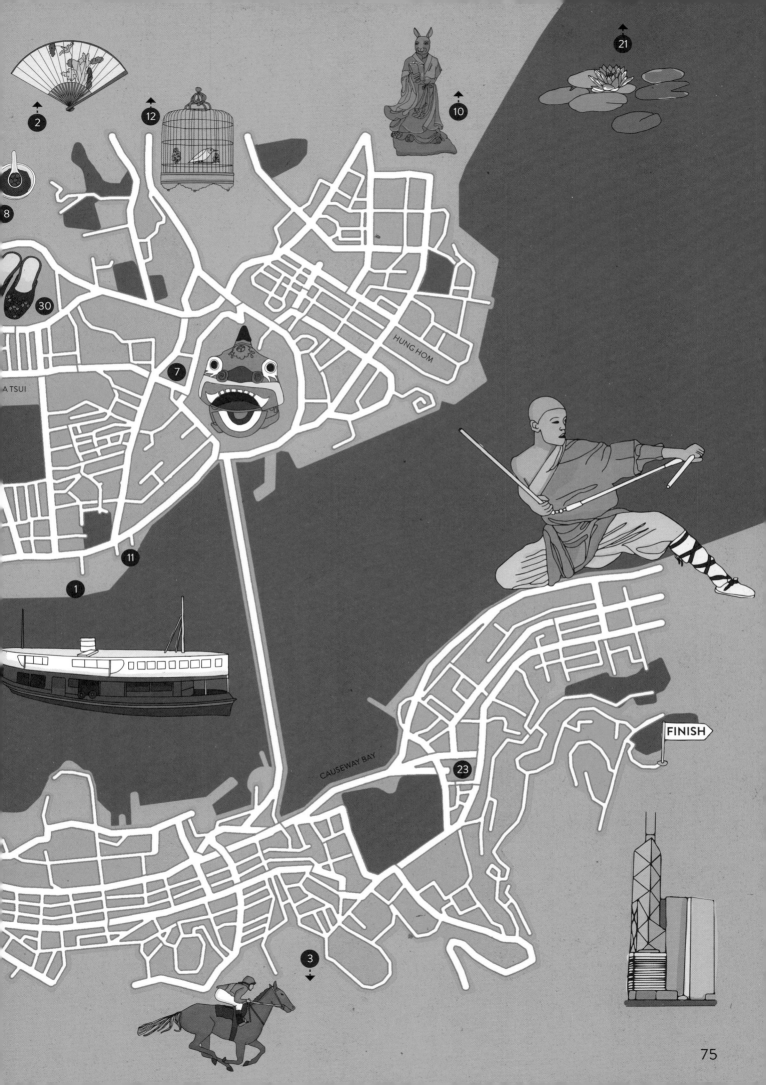

HONG KONG

Hong Kong welcomes visitors with its iconic skyline, an array of the world's smoothest transport systems and a legendary kitchen; whether the deliciousness in the pot is Cantonese, Sichuanese, Japanese or French. Behind the city's futuristic façade hide smoky temples, surf-beaten beaches and sprawling country parks filled with protected wildlife.

(1) STAR FERRY

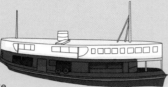

You can't say you've 'done' Hong Kong until you've taken a ride on a Star Ferry, that wonderful fleet of electric-diesel vessels with names like *Celestial Star* and *Twinkling Star*.

(2) LADIES' MARKET

The Tung Choi Street market is a cheek-by-jowl affair offering cheap clothes and trinkets in the afternoons. A terrific place to soak up local atmosphere.

(3) HAPPY VALLEY RACECOURSE
www.hkjc.com/home/english/index.asp

An outing at the races is one of the quintessential Hong Kong things to do, especially if you happen to be around during one of the weekly Wednesday evening races here. The atmosphere is electric.

(4) MAK'S NOODLES

At this legendary shop, noodles are made the traditional way with a bamboo pole and served perched on a spoon placed over the bowl so they won't go soggy. The beef brisket noodles are equally remarkable.

(5) CENTRAL–MID-LEVELS ESCALATOR

The world's longest covered outdoor people-mover zigzags from Central's offices to homes near Conduit Rd. Embark and let the streets unveil themselves.

(6) HSBC BUILDING

This stunning building is a masterpiece of precision and innovation. And so it should be; on completion in 1985, it was the world's most expensive building. Don't miss the bronze lions guarding the harbour-side entrance. Rub their paws for luck.

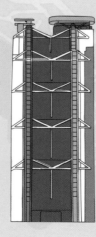

(7) HONG KONG MUSEUM OF HISTORY
www.hk.history.museum

For a whistle-stop overview of the territory's archaeology, ethnography, and natural and local history, this museum is well worth a visit, not just to learn more about the subject, but also to understand how Hong Kong presents its stories to the world.

(8) SHANGHAI STREET

Strolling down Shanghai Street will take you back to a time long past. Once Kowloon's main drag, it's flanked by stores selling Chinese wedding gowns, sandalwood incense and Buddha statues, as well as mah-jong parlours and an old pawn shop.

(9) PENINSULA HONG KONG
www.peninsula.com

The Peninsula (c1928), housed in a throne-like building, is one of the world's great hotels. Taking afternoon tea here is a wonderful experience – dress neatly and be prepared to queue for a table.

(10) SIK SIK YUEN WONG TAI SIN TEMPLE
www.siksikyuen.org.hk

An explosion of colourful pillars, roofs, lattice work, flowers and incense, this busy temple is a destination for all walks of Hong Kong society, from pensioners and business people to parents and young professionals.

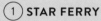

(11) TSIM SHA TSUI EAST PROMENADE

This promenade offers an uninterrupted view of one of the finest city skylines in the world. It really comes into its own in the evening, during the nightly Symphony of Lights sound-and-light show.

(12) YUEN PO STREET BIRD GARDEN AND FLOWER MARKET

In this enchanting corner of Mong Kok, a handful of old men can be found 'walking' their caged songbirds. There are also feathered creatures for sale, along with elaborately carved cages. The flower market is adjacent.

(13) CITY HALL MAXIM'S PALACE

This 'palace' offers the quintessential Hong Kong dim sum experience. It's cheerful, it's noisy and it takes place in a huge kitschy hall with dragon decorations and hundreds of locals. A dizzying assortment of dim sum is paraded on trolleys the old-fashioned way.

(14) ANGEL'S SHARE WHISKY BAR
www.angelsshare.hk

One of Hong Kong's best whisky bars, this clubby place has more than 100 whiskies from the world over – predominantly Scottish, but also French, Japanese and American. If you're hungry, there's a selection of whisky-inspired dishes.

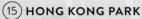

15 HONG KONG PARK

Hong Kong Park is one of the most unusual parks in the world, with artificial creations such as its fountain plaza, conservatory, waterfall, indoor games hall, playground, taichi garden, viewing tower, museum and arts centre.

16 MAN MO TEMPLE

One of Hong Kong's oldest temples and a declared monument, atmospheric Man Mo Temple is dedicated to the gods of literature ('Man'), holding a writing brush, and of war ('Mo'), wielding a sword.

17 VICTORIA PEAK

www.thepeak.com.hk

Standing at 552m, the Peak is one of the most visited spots by tourists in Hong Kong for the sweeping views of the metropolis, verdant woods and easy, but spectacular, walks.

18 TEMPLE STREET NIGHT MARKET

The liveliest night market in Hong Kong, Temple Street is a good place to go for the bustling atmosphere and the smells and tastes of the *dai pai dong* (open-air street stall) food.

19 PEAK TRAM

www.thepeak.com.hk

A ride on the Peak Tram has been a classic Hong Kong experience since 1888, with vertiginous views over the city as you ascend up the steep mountainside.

20 ABERDEEN PROMENADE

Tree-lined Aberdeen Promenade runs from sprawling Aberdeen Wholesale Fish Market past berthed house boats and seafood-processing vessels to the market.

21 CHI LIN NUNNERY

www.chilin.org

One of the most beautiful and arrestingly built environments in Hong Kong, this large Buddhist complex is a serene place, with lotus ponds, immaculate bonsai tea plants, bougainvillea and silent nuns.

22 THE POTTINGER

www.thepottinger.com

Smack in the heart of Central, this unobtrusive boutique hotel has 86 airy, white and cream rooms with subtle Asian touches – carved wooden screens, calligraphy work, and black and white photos of old Hong Kong.

23 TUVE

www.tuve.hk

From the dungeon-like entrance to the noir-ish reception area with black iron grille and the brass-and-concrete slab that is the front desk, everything at this hotel spells industrial-style design.

24 HELENA MAY

www.helenamay.com

Founded in 1916 as a social club for single European women, this is now a private club for women of all nationalities, and a hotel with 43 creaky, but charming, rooms.

25 LUNG KING HEEN

www.fourseasons.com/hongkong

This is the world's first Chinese restaurant to receive three Michelin stars. The Cantonese food is excellent in both taste and presentation; combined with the harbour views, it provides a truly stellar dining experience.

26 ABERDEEN FISH MARKET YEE HOPE SEAFOOD RESTAURANT

Hidden in Hong Kong's only wholesale fish market, this understated eatery run by fishers is truly an in-the-know place for ultrafresh seafood. Tell them your budget and they'll source the best sea creatures available.

27 LUK YU TEA HOUSE

This gorgeous tea house (c1933), known for its masterful cooking and Eastern art deco decor, was the haunt of opera artists, writers and painters, who came to give recitals and discuss the national fate.

28 PMQ

www.pmq.org.hk

The modernist building that was once the police married quarters is now one of the best places in Hong Kong to shop for pieces by local designers, jewellery makers and artisans.

29 G.O.D.

www.god.com.hk

One of the coolest born-in-Hong Kong shops around, G.O.D. does irreverent takes on classic Hong Kong iconography. Think mobile phone covers printed with pictures of Hong Kong housing blocks.

30 YUE HWA CHINESE PRODUCTS EMPORIUM

www.yuehwa.com

This five-storey behemoth is one of the few old-school Chinese department stores left in the city. You'll find silk scarves, traditional Chinese baby clothes and embroidered slippers.

BĚIJĪNG

Complex and compelling, Běijīng is often a stop
on the way to the Great Wall, but there is so much
more to this city. Join the crowds and pedal
your way from west to east.

1. FORBIDDEN CITY
2. TIĀN'ĀNMÉN SQUARE
3. SUMMER PALACE
4. TEMPLE OF HEAVEN
5. LAMA TEMPLE
6. BELL TOWER
7. NATIONAL MUSEUM OF CHINA
8. LONG CORRIDOR (SUMMER PALACE)
9. MIÀOYĪNG TEMPLE WHITE DAGOBA
10. CONFUCIUS TEMPLE &
    IMPERIAL COLLEGE
11. GALAXY SOHO
12. HALL OF CLOCKS & WATCHES
    (FORBIDDEN CITY)
13. HÒUHǍI LAKES
14. CHINA NUMISMATIC MUSEUM
15. MING TOMBS
16. GRACELAND YARD
17. AMAN AT SUMMER PALACE
18. TEMPLE HOTEL
19. ROSEWOOD BĚIJĪNG
20. 4CORNERS
21. LOST HEAVEN
22. POTTERY WORKSHOP
23. JĪNGZŪN PEKING DUCK
24. PĀNJIĀYUÁN MARKET
25. PLASTERED 8
26. SLOW LANE
27. GOLDEN PEACOCK
28. MEI LANFANG GRAND THEATRE
29. CHAIRMAN MAO MEMORIAL HALL
30. RUÌFÚXIÁNG

FINISH

GULOU

SĀNLĪTÚN

DONGCHEN

CHÁOYÁNG

XICHENG

DASHILAN

BĚIJĪNG

Constantly reimagining itself as it races towards the future, yet inextricably linked to its glorious, notorious past, Běijīng is as compelling as it is complex. The dazzling array of different dishes you'll encounter reflects the sheer joy locals take in eating, and few places on earth can match the extraordinary historical panorama on display. With top-class museums, galleries and tumbling acrobats galore, Běijīng has more than enough to keep you busy.

① FORBIDDEN CITY

www.dpm.org.cn

Ringed by a 52m-wide moat at the very heart of Běijīng, the Forbidden City is China's largest and best-preserved collection of ancient buildings, and the largest palace complex in the world.

② TIĀN'ĀNMÉN SQUARE

Flanked by stern 1950s Soviet-style buildings and ringed by white perimeter fences, the world's largest public square (440,000 sq metres) is an immense flatland of paving stones.

③ SUMMER PALACE

The Summer Palace was the playground for emperors fleeing the suffocating summer torpor of the old imperial city. A marvel of design, it offers an escape into the landscapes of traditional Chinese painting.

④ TEMPLE OF HEAVEN

A tranquil oasis of peace and methodical Confucian design in one of China's busiest urban landscapes, the 267-hectare Temple of Heaven Park was originally a stage for solemn rites performed by the emperor.

⑤ LAMA TEMPLE

www.yonghegong.cn

This exceptional temple is a glittering attraction in Běijīng's Buddhist firmament. If you only have time for one temple, make it this one, where superb Chinese lions mingle with dense clouds of incense.

⑥ BELL TOWER

The modest, grey-stone structure of the Bell Tower is arguably more charming than its resplendent other half, the Drum Tower, and it also allows travellers to view its sister tower from a balcony.

⑦ NATIONAL MUSEUM OF CHINA

www.en.chnmuseum.cn

Běijīng's premier museum is housed in an immense 1950s communist-style building on the eastern side of Tiān'ānmén Square, and is well worth visiting: the Ancient China exhibition is outstanding.

⑧ LONG CORRIDOR (SUMMER PALACE)

Perhaps the premier sight of the Summer Palace, this corridor stretches for almost half a mile and is covered in 14,000 intricate paintings depicting scenes from Chinese history and myths.

⑨ MIÀOYĪNG TEMPLE WHITE DAGOBA

Originally built in 1271, the serene Miàoyīng Temple slumbers beneath its huge, distinctive, chalk-white Yuan dynasty pagoda, which towers over the surrounding *hútòng* (alleys). Even today it is the tallest Tibetan-style pagoda in China.

⑩ CONFUCIUS TEMPLE & IMPERIAL COLLEGE

An almost otherworldly sense of detachment is impossible to shift at China's second-largest Confucian temple. In its tranquillity and reserve, the temple can be a pleasant sanctuary from Běijīng's congested streets.

⑪ GALAXY SOHO

Běijīng's striking Galaxy Soho building announces itself as one of the capital's modern architectural landmarks. Opened in 2012, it stands in direct juxtaposition to the adjoining *hútòng* housing (which, controversially, was cleared for its development).

⑫ HALL OF CLOCKS & WATCHES (FORBIDDEN CITY)

The Clock Exhibition Hall is one of the highlights of the Forbidden City. The exhibition contains an astonishing array of elaborate timepieces, many of which were gifts to the Qing emperors from overseas.

⑬ HÒUHĂI LAKES

The Hòuhăi Lakes are comprised of three lakes: Qiánhăi (Front Lake), Hòuhăi (Back Lake) and Xīhăi (West Lake). Together they are one of the capital's favourite outdoor spots.

⑭ CHINA NUMISMATIC MUSEUM

Located in a former 1930s bank, this museum follows the evolution of money production in China. You'll see spade-shaped coins, chunky gold-nugget coins and 'money necklaces' containing strings of small bronze knives.

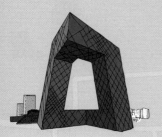

15 MING TOMBS

The Ming Tombs are the final resting place of 13 of the 16 Ming emperors. Explore ceremonial tomb architecture and the 'sacred way' lined with statues of humans and animals.

16 GRACELAND YARD

www.graceland-yardhotel.com

Graceland is an exquisitely renovated courtyard hotel, housed within the grounds of the abandoned, 500-year-old Zhèngjué Temple. Each of the eight rooms is slightly different, using traditional Buddhist-themed furnishings.

17 AMAN AT SUMMER PALACE

www.amanresorts.com

Hard to fault this exquisite hotel, a candidate for the best in Běijīng. Parts of the hotel date to the 19th century and were used to house distinguished guests waiting for audiences with Empress Cixi.

18 TEMPLE HOTEL

www.thetemplehotel.com

This unique heritage hotel forms part of a renovation project that was recognised by Unesco for its conservation efforts. A team spent five years renovating a part-abandoned 250-year-old Buddhist temple.

19 ROSEWOOD BĚIJĪNG

www.rosewoodhotels.com/en/beijing

The elegant hotel Rosewood fits modern luxury within a traditional Chinese design, incorporating decorative arts and a subtle yin-and-yang theme. Its entry is guarded by two large Jiao Tu (Sons of Dragon) sculptures.

20 4CORNERS

www.these4corners.com

Given this *hútòng* bar-restaurant is run by a Canadian-Vietnamese expat, it makes total sense that it's known for its *pho* and *poutine*. Its courtyard bar is one of the area's best spots for a drink.

21 LOST HEAVEN

www.lostheaven.com.cn

The Běijīng branch of the famed Shànghǎi restaurant, Lost Heaven specialises in the folk cuisine of Yúnnán province. While the spices have been toned down, the flavours are guaranteed to transport you to China's balmy southwest.

22 POTTERY WORKSHOP

Featuring the work from a collective of six young artists, this wonderful yet small ceramics store has a beautiful range of handmade, hand-painted teacups, teasets, vases and incense-holders.

23 JĪNGZŪN PEKING DUCK

A very popular place to sample Běijīng's signature dish. Not only is the Peking duck here extremely good value, you can also sit outside on the atmospheric wooden-decked terrace, decorated with red lanterns.

24 PĀNJIĀYUÁN MARKET

Hands down the best place in Běijīng to shop for *yìshù* (arts), *gōngyì* (crafts) and *gǔwán* (antiques). Some stalls open every day, but the market is at its biggest and most lively on weekends.

25 PLASTERED 8

www.plasteredtshirts.com

British-owned, this iconic Nanluogu Xiang T-shirt shop prints ironic takes on Chinese culture onto its good-quality T-shirts and tops. Also stocks decent smog masks.

26 SLOW LANE

Secreted away down historic Shijia Hutong, this quietly seductive shop sells beautiful, handmade teaware and quality tea, as well as elegant clothing, much of which is made from Tibetan yak wool.

27 GOLDEN PEACOCK

Make sure you try the pineapple rice and the tangy dried beef at this unpretentious and popular restaurant, which specialises in the cuisine of the Dǎi people from southwest China.

28 MEI LANFANG GRAND THEATRE

www.bjmlfdjy.cn

Named after China's most famous practitioner of Peking opera, this theatre opened its doors in 2007 and has since become one of the most popular and versatile venues in town.

29 CHAIRMAN MAO MEMORIAL HALL

One of Běijīng's more surreal spectacles is the sight of Mao Zedong's embalmed corpse on public display within his mausoleum. The Soviet-inspired memorial hall was constructed soon after Mao died in September 1976.

30 RUÌFÚXIÁNG

The store Ruìfúxiáng has been trading since 1893 and is one of the best places in town to browse for silk. There's an incredible selection of Shāndōng silk, brocade and satin-silk.

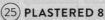

SEOUL

With so much to experience in this dynamic city
– from temples to technology and mountain trails –
will you ever reach your final destination?

JONGNO-GU

YONGSAN-GU

FINISH

1. DONGDAEMUN DESIGN PLAZA & PARK
2. LOTTE WORLD
3. DEOKSUGUNG
4. NAMDAEMUN MARKET
5. CHANGDEOKGUNG
6. JOGYE-SA
7. GYEONGBOKGUNG
8. NATIONAL MUSEUM OF KOREA
9. OLYMPIC PARK
10. WAR MEMORIAL OF KOREA
11. BANK OF KOREA MONEY MUSEUM
12. SEODAEMUN PRISON HISTORY HALL
13. MULLAE ARTS VILLAGE
14. KOREA FURNITURE MUSEUM
15. ITAEWON BUGUNDANG HISTORY PARK

DONGDAEMUN-GU

SEONGDONG-GU

GWANGJIN-GU

18

START

9

25

2

16. AGRICULTURE MUSEUM
17. STAIRWAY FLEA MARKET
18. SEOUL YANGNYEONGSI HERB MEDICINE MUSEUM
19. WAR AND WOMEN'S HUMAN RIGHTS MUSEUM
20. URBANWOOD GUESTHOUSE

21. ITAEWON G GUEST HOUSE
22. HOTEL THE DESIGNERS
23. SMALL HOUSE BIG DOOR
24. MINARI HOUSE
25. PARK HYATT SEOUL

26. RAK-KO-JAE
27. GWANGJANG MARKET
28. MENYA SANDAIME
29. PHO FOR YOU
30. ROOT

SEOUL

Fashion- and technology-forward, but also deeply traditional, this dynamic city mashes up temples, palaces, cutting-edge design and mountain trails, all to a nonstop K-Pop beat. Whatever you want, at any time of day or night, Seoul can provide. An early-morning temple visit can lead to a palace tour followed by tea-sipping in Bukchon and gallery-hopping in Samcheong-dong.

① DONGDAEMUN DESIGN PLAZA & PARK
www.ddp.or.kr

Zaha Hadid's building, a curvaceous concrete structure with a silvery façade partly coated with lawns that rise up on to its roof, is a showcase for Korean and international design.

② LOTTE WORLD

This huge complex includes an amusement park, an ice-skating rink, a cinema multiplex, department store, folk museum, shopping mall, hotel, restaurants and more. Kids and adults alike will love the place.

③ DEOKSUGUNG
www.deoksugung.go.kr

Deoksugung (meaning Palace of Virtuous Longevity) is the only Seoul palace that you can visit in the evening and see the buildings illuminated. It first served as a palace in 1593.

④ NAMDAEMUN MARKET
www.namdaemunmarket.co.kr

You could spend all day in this swarming night-and-day market and not see it at all. The largest market in Korea, each section has hundreds of stalls; its food market is the biggest highlight.

⑤ CHANGDEOKGUNG
eng.cdg.go.kr/main/main.htm

You must join a guided tour to look around World Heritage-listed Changdeokgung, the most beautiful of Seoul's five main palaces.

⑥ JOGYE-SA
www.jogyesa.kr/user/english

The focus of temple Jogye-sa is the giant wooden hall Daeungjeon, Seoul's largest Buddhist worship hall. Completed in 1938, its exterior is decorated with scenes from Buddha's life, while inside are three giant Buddha statues.

⑦ GYEONGBOKGUNG
www.royalpalace.go.kr

At Seoul's premier palace, watch the changing of the guard ceremonies at the main entrance Gwanghwamun, then set aside at least half a day to do justice to the compound.

⑧ NATIONAL MUSEUM OF KOREA
www.museum.go.kr

The grand, marble-lined, modernist building cleverly channels plenty of natural light to show off Korea's ancient treasures. Among the must-see exhibits are the Golden Treasures for the Great Tomb of Hwangham.

⑨ OLYMPIC PARK
www.olympicpark.co.kr

This large and pleasant park was the focus of the 1988 Olympics. Strolling its paths takes you past its stadiums surrounded by greenery, ponds and open-air sculptures.

⑩ WAR MEMORIAL OF KOREA
www.warmemo.co.kr

This huge museum documents the history of the Korean War (1950–53) with black and white documentary footage of the main battles and events, plus plenty of military hardware outside.

⑪ BANK OF KOREA MONEY MUSEUM
museum.bok.or.kr

Built in 1912, and an outstanding example of Japanese colonial architecture, the old Bank of Korea now houses an interesting exhibition on the history of local and foreign currency.

⑫ SEODAEMUN PRISON HISTORY HALL
www.sscmc.or.kr/culture2/foreign/eng/eng01.html

This one-time prison is a symbol of Japanese cruelty and oppression during their rule of Korea (1910–45). It was also used by Korea's various postwar dictators up until its closure in 1987.

⑬ MULLAE ARTS VILLAGE

Something very interesting is going on in Mullae-dong, a light-industrial area of the city packed with compact metalwork factories. Artists and designers have moved in beside the steel workers and welders.

⑭ KOREA FURNITURE MUSEUM
www.kofum.com

Advanced reservations are required to tour this gem of a museum, whose collection includes furniture made from wood like persimmon, maple and paulownia, some decorated with lacquer, mother of pearl or tortoise shell.

⑮ ITAEWON BUGUNDANG HISTORY PARK

Located atop a hill directly facing N Seoul Tower, inside the park is a monument dedicated to Korean Christian freedom fighter Yu Gwan-sun, as well as Bugundang Shrine, which dates back to 1619.

⑯ AGRICULTURE MUSEUM

Much more interesting than it sounds, this museum has imaginative displays that relate to the history and practice of farming on the Korean peninsula, as well as general aspects of traditional rural life.

⑰ STAIRWAY FLEA MARKET

Held the last Saturday of each month, the market is on top of Itaewon Hill, where local artists sell their works on the street lined with studios, galleries, pop-up shops, bars and eateries.

⑱ SEOUL YANGNYEONGSI HERB MEDICINE MUSEUM
museum.ddm.go.kr

Learn about the history and practice of traditional Korean medicine at this imaginative museum. The kind staff here serve herbal tea and allow you to work out which *sasang* (constitution) you have.

⑲ WAR AND WOMEN'S HUMAN RIGHTS MUSEUM
www.womenandwar.net

When you enter this well-designed and powerful museum, you'll be given the story of a *halmoni* (WWII 'comfort women') helping you to connect with the tragic history of these women in sexual slavery.

⑳ URBANWOOD GUESTHOUSE
www.urbanwood.co.kr

Creatively decorated in bright colours and modern furnishings, this cosy guesthouse feels more like a cool arty apartment. Martin, the convivial English-speaking host, knows the area well and makes a mean coffee.

㉑ ITAEWON G GUEST HOUSE
www.gguest.com

This hostel stands above others for its attention to thought and detail. Set in a renovated industrial-chic apartment building, its private rooms and dorms are clean, spacious and have quality thick mattresses.

㉒ HOTEL THE DESIGNERS
www.hotelthedesigners.com

Eighteen designers were given free reign to decorate the suites at this sophisticated love motel, tucked off the main road. Check the website to browse the different themes.

㉓ SMALL HOUSE BIG DOOR
www.smallhousebigdoor.com

This suave little art hotel is quite the find. Its white-toned rooms all feature locally designed, handmade furniture and beds, and maximise the use of space with ingenious slide-out desks and TVs.

㉔ MINARI HOUSE
www.minarihouse.com

Designed as a base for artists and creatives, the four appealing rooms at this guesthouse sport minimalist design and arty touches. Breakfast is served in a lovely gallery cafe, which opens onto a garden.

㉕ PARK HYATT SEOUL
www.seoul.grand.hyatt.com/en/hotel/home.html

A discrete entrance to this hotel – look for the rock sticking out of the wall – sets the Zen-minimalist tone for the gorgeous property. Each floor only has 10 rooms with spot-lit antiquities lining the hallways.

㉖ RAK-KO-JAE
www.rkj.co.kr

This beautifully restored *hanok*, with an enchanting garden is modelled after Japan's *ryokan*. The guesthouse's mud-walled sauna is included in the prices, as is breakfast and dinner.

㉗ GWANGJANG MARKET
www.kwangjangmarket.co.kr

Best known as Seoul's largest food alley (or *meokjagolmok*), the Gwangjang Market is home to some 200 stalls among *kimchi* and seafood vendors. Its speciality is the golden-fried *nokdu bindaetteok* (mung-bean pancake).

㉘ MENYA SANDAIME
www.menyasandaime.com

This atmospheric ramen shop is a great place for single diners, who can sit at the counter by the open kitchen watching the hip, tattooed chefs carefully craft bowls of delicious noodles.

㉙ PHO FOR YOU

This restaurant serves Vietnamese classics, such as *banh mi* and beef *bun bo*, and the appetiser sets are among Seoul's best; the dish to order here is certainly the San Francisco-style *pho*.

㉚ ROOT

Not only does Root restaurant boast some of the best salads, soups and sandwiches in Seoul, it does it with fresh ingredients, a full flavour profile and a splash of Asian flavour.

KYOTO

Kyoto is old Japan writ large: over 1000 quiet temples, sublime gardens, colourful shrines and geisha scurrying to secret liaisons. Few cities of this size offer such a range of excellent restaurants, many in traditional wooden buildings. Here you can visit an old *shōtengai* (market street) and admire an array of ancient speciality shops: tofu sellers, *washi* (Japanese handmade paper) stores and tea merchants.

KAMIGYO WARD

NAKAGYO WARD

SHIMOGYO WARD

MINAMI WARD

① TŌFUKU-JI
Home to a spectacular garden, several superb structures and beautiful precincts, Tōfuku-ji is one of the best temples in Kyoto.

② NANZEN-JI
www.nanzenji.com
This rewarding temple offers expansive grounds and numerous sub-temples. Steps lead up to the second storey, which has a great view over the city.

③ KYOTO IMPERIAL PALACE
www.kunaicho.go.jp
The Kyoto Imperial Palace, known as the Gosho in Japanese, is a walled complex that sits in the middle of the Kyoto Imperial Palace Park.

④ CHION-IN
www.chion-in.or.jp
A collection of soaring buildings and spacious courtyards, Chion-in serves as the headquarters of the Jōdo sect, the largest school of Buddhism in Japan.

⑦ GION

Gion is the famous entertainment and geisha quarter on the Kamo-gawa's eastern bank. Best experienced today on an evening stroll past the 17th-century traditional restaurants and teahouses.

⑧ NISHIKI MARKET

Head to the covered Nishiki Market to check out the weird and wonderful foods that go into Kyoto cuisine, like squid skewers, barrels of *tsukemono* (pickled vegetables), cute sweets, wasabi salt and *yakitori* skewers.

⑨ NIJŌ-JŌ

The military might of Japan's great warlord generals, the Tokugawa shoguns, is amply demonstrated by the imposing stone walls and ramparts of their great castle, Nijō-jō, which dominates a large part of Northwest Kyoto.

⑩ TAWARAYA

Hotel Tawaraya has been operating for more than three centuries and is one of the finest places to stay in the world. It's arguably one of the best *ryokans* (traditional Japanese inns) available, from decorations to service to food.

⑪ LOWER EAST 9 HOSTEL

www.lowereastnine.com

LE9 is a design-savvy hostel in a quiet spot south of Kyoto Station. Dorms are spacious capsule-style with thoughtful details, while the twin private rooms come with a private bathroom.

⑫ ARASHIYAMA BAMBOO GROVE

Walking into this extensive bamboo grove is like entering another world – the thick green bamboo stalks seem to continue endlessly in every direction and there's a strange quality to the light.

⑬ ICHIZAWA SHINZABURO HANPU

www.ichizawa.co.jp

This company has been making its canvas bags for more than 110 years and the store is often crammed with those in the know picking up a skillfully crafted Kyoto product.

⑭ IPPŌDŌ TEA

www.ippodo-tea.co.jp

This old-style shop sells some of the best Japanese tea in Kyoto, and you'll be given an English leaflet with tea prices and descriptions. Its *matcha* makes an excellent and lightweight souvenir.

⑮ KŌBŌ-SAN MARKET

This market is held at Tō-ji each month to commemorate the death of a former abbot. If you're after used kimonos, pottery, bric-a-brac, plants, tools and general Japanalia, this is the place.

⑤ HEIAN-JINGŪ

One of Kyoto's more popular sights, this shrine was built in 1895 to commemorate the 1100th anniversary of the founding of the city.

⑥ FUSHIMI INARI-TAISHA SHINTO

With seemingly endless arcades of vermilion *torii* (shrine gates) spread across a thickly wooded mountain, this vast shrine complex is one of the most impressive and memorable sights in all of Kyoto.

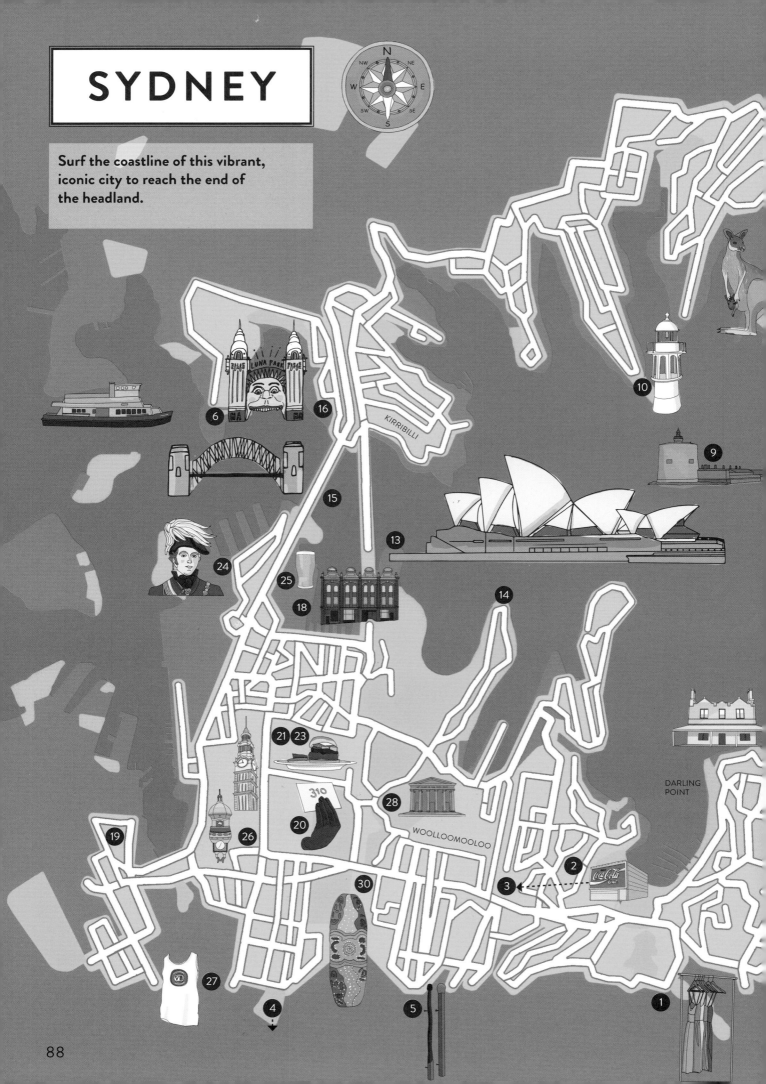

Surf the coastline of this vibrant, iconic city to reach the end of the headland.

KIRRIBILLI

DARLING POINT

WOOLLOOMOOLOO

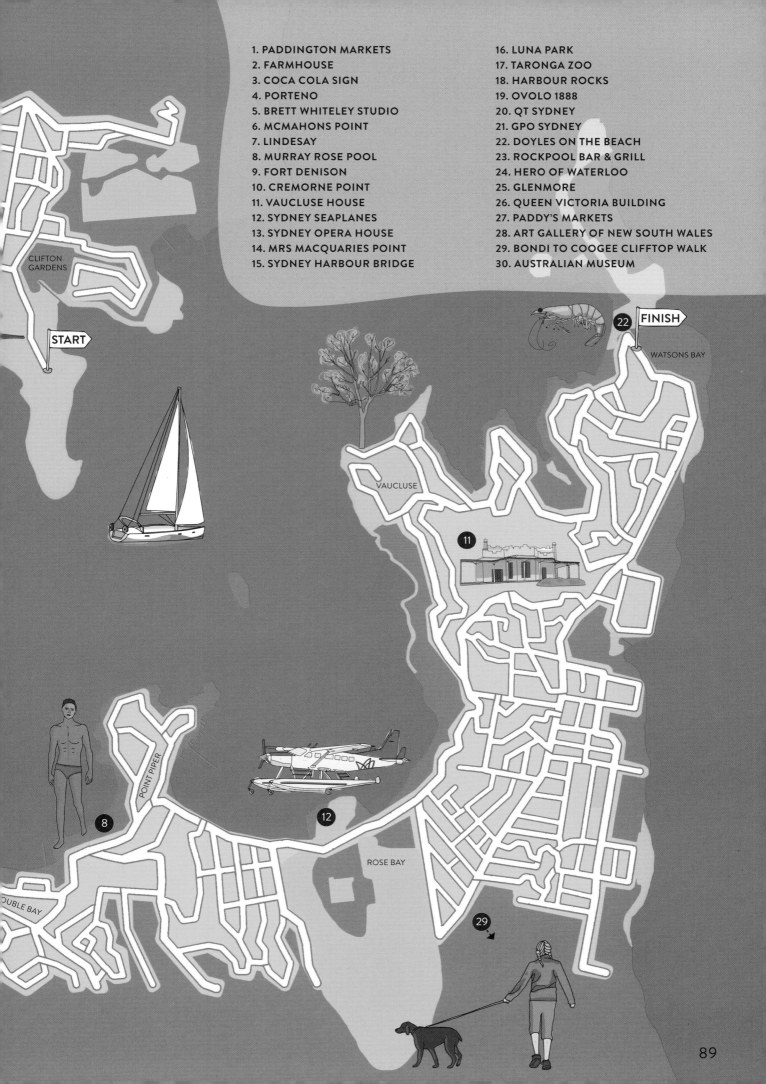

1. PADDINGTON MARKETS
2. FARMHOUSE
3. COCA COLA SIGN
4. PORTENO
5. BRETT WHITELEY STUDIO
6. MCMAHONS POINT
7. LINDESAY
8. MURRAY ROSE POOL
9. FORT DENISON
10. CREMORNE POINT
11. VAUCLUSE HOUSE
12. SYDNEY SEAPLANES
13. SYDNEY OPERA HOUSE
14. MRS MACQUARIES POINT
15. SYDNEY HARBOUR BRIDGE
16. LUNA PARK
17. TARONGA ZOO
18. HARBOUR ROCKS
19. OVOLO 1888
20. QT SYDNEY
21. GPO SYDNEY
22. DOYLES ON THE BEACH
23. ROCKPOOL BAR & GRILL
24. HERO OF WATERLOO
25. GLENMORE
26. QUEEN VICTORIA BUILDING
27. PADDY'S MARKETS
28. ART GALLERY OF NEW SOUTH WALES
29. BONDI TO COOGEE CLIFFTOP WALK
30. AUSTRALIAN MUSEUM

CLIFTON GARDENS

START

FINISH

WATSONS BAY

VAUCLUSE

POINT PIPER

ROSE BAY

DOUBLE BAY

SYDNEY

Day or night, this city sure is good-looking. Defined by its rugged Pacific coastline and exquisite harbour, Sydney relies on its coastal setting to replenish its reserves of charm. Large chunks of the harbour are still edged with bush, while parks cut their way through the skyscrapers. After a lazy day at the beach, there's always a new restaurant to try, undercover bar to hunt down, hip band to check out, sports team to shout at, show or party to attend.

1 PADDINGTON MARKETS

Originating in the 1970s, when they were drenched in the scent of patchouli oil, these markets are considerably more mainstream these days. They're still worth exploring for their new and vintage clothing, crafts and jewellery.

2 FARMHOUSE

Occupying a space between restaurant and supper club, this place has a tiny kitchen and a charming host. Diners sit at a long table and eat a set menu of uncomplicated, delicious dishes from high-quality produce.

3 COCA COLA SIGN

A Sydney landmark, this huge sign marks the entrance to Kings Cross. You're actually looking at the 2016 model: the previous one was replaced, then auctioned off letter by letter for local homeless charity the Wayside Chapel.

4 PORTENO

This upbeat and deservedly acclaimed Argentine restaurant is a great place to eat. The 'animal of the day' is slow-roasted for eight hours before the doors even open and is always delicious.

5 BRETT WHITELEY STUDIO

www.artgallery.nsw.gov.au/brett-whiteley-studio
Acclaimed local artist Brett Whiteley lived fast and without restraint. His studio has been preserved as a gallery for some of his best work. Pride of place goes to his astonishing 'Alchemy', a giant multi-panel extravaganza that could absorb you for hours.

6 MCMAHONS POINT

Is there a better view of the Bridge and the Opera House than from the wharf at this point, a short hop by ferry northwest of the centre? It's all unfolded before you and is a stunning spot to be when the sun is setting.

7 LINDESAY

Lindesay is rarely open, but, aside from Nicole Kidman inviting you in for tea, this is probably your best chance to look inside an actual Darling Point mansion. Built in 1834, it's still got its Georgian interiors, servants' quarters and long lawn overlooking the harbour.

8 MURRAY ROSE POOL

Not really a pool at all, family-friendly Murray Rose (named after a champion Olympic swimmer) is a large, shark-netted enclosure that is one of the harbour's best swimming spots. As the closest swimming spot to the city, it attracts an urbane cross-section of inner-eastern locals.

9 FORT DENISON

In colonial times this small fortified harbour island was a sorry site of suffering, used to isolate recalcitrant convicts and nicknamed 'Pinchgut' for its meagre rations. Fears of a Russian invasion during the Crimean War led to its fortification.

10 CREMORNE POINT

Cremorne Point is a beautiful spot for a picnic on grassy Cremorne Reserve, or for a swim in the free saltwater MacCallum Pool. The harbour views from here are downright delicious (especially when the New Year's Eve fireworks are erupting).

11 VAUCLUSE HOUSE

Construction of this imposing, turreted specimen of Gothic Australiana, set amid 25 ares of lush gardens, commenced in 1805, but the house was tinkered with into the 1860s. Decorated with beautiful European period pieces, Vaucluse House offers visitors a rare glimpse into early well-to-do Sydney colonial life.

12 SYDNEY SEAPLANES

Based very near Rose Bay ferry wharf, this company offers scenic flights around Sydney Harbour and beaches. Aerial excitement meets epicurean delight when you take a seaplane flight to a secluded seafood restaurant such as the Berowra Waters Inn.

13 SYDNEY OPERA HOUSE

www.sydneyoperahouse.com
Designed by Danish architect Jørn Utzon, this World Heritage-listed building is Australia's most recognisable landmark. Visually referencing a yacht's billowing white sails, it's a soaring, commanding presence on the harbour.

14 MRS MACQUARIES POINT

Mrs Macquaries Point forms the northeastern tip of Farm Cove and provides beautiful views over the bay to the Opera House and city skyline.

15 SYDNEY HARBOUR BRIDGE

Sydneysiders adore their giant 'coathanger'. Opened in 1932, this majestic structure spans the harbour at one of its narrowest points, and the best way to experience it is on foot.

16 LUNA PARK

www.lunaparksydney.com

A sinister chip-toothed clown face forms the entrance to this old-fashioned amusement park overlooking Sydney Harbour. It's one of several 1930s features, including the Coney Island funhouse and a pretty carousel.

17 TARONGA ZOO

www.taronga.org.au

This bushy harbour hillside is full of kangaroos, koalas and similarly hirsute Australians, plus numerous imported guests. The zoo's critters have million-dollar harbour views, but seem blissfully unaware of the privilege.

18 HARBOUR ROCKS

www.harbourrocks.com.au

This boutique hotel has undergone a chic transformation from colonial warehouse and workers' cottages to a series of loft-style rooms with high ceilings, distressed brick and elegant furnishings.

19 OVOLO 1888

www.ovolohotels.com

In a heritage-listed wool store, this stylish gem combines industrial minimalism with the warmth of ironbark wood beams, luxury appointments and engaged staff.

20 QT SYDNEY

www.qtsydney.com.au

Fun, sexy and relaxed, this ultra-theatrical, effortlessly cool hotel is located in the historic State Theatre. Art-deco eccentricity is complemented by quirky extras in the rooms.

21 GPO SYDNEY

www.gpograncl.com

This beautiful colonnaded sandstone Victorian palazzo (built 1874) was once Sydney's General Post Office. It has since been transformed into the Westin Sydney hotel, swanky shops, restaurants and bars.

22 DOYLES ON THE BEACH

www.doyles.com.au

There may well be better places for seafood, but few can compete with Doyles' location or its history. Catching the harbour ferry to Watsons Bay for a seafood lunch is a quintessential Sydney experience.

23 ROCKPOOL BAR & GRILL

www.rockpool.com

This sleek operation in the art-deco City Mutual Building is famous for its dry-aged, full-blood Wagyu burger (make sure you order a side of the hand-cut fat chips).

24 HERO OF WATERLOO

www.heroofwaterloo.com.au

Enter this rough-hewn 1843 sandstone pub to meet some locals, chat up the Irish bar staff and grab an earful of the swing, folk and Celtic bands.

25 GLENMORE

www.theglenmore.com.au

Downstairs it's a predictably nice old Rocks pub, but head up to the rooftop and the views are beyond fabulous: Opera House, harbour and city skyline all present and accounted for.

26 QUEEN VICTORIA BUILDING

www.qvb.com.au

The magnificent QVB takes up a whole block and boasts nearly 200 shops on five levels. It's a High Victorian masterpiece – without doubt Sydney's most beautiful shopping centre.

27 PADDY'S MARKETS

www.paddysmarkets.com.au

Cavernous, 1000-stall Paddy's is the Sydney equivalent of Istanbul's Grand Bazaar. Pick up a VB singlet for Uncle Bruce or wander the aisles in capitalist awe.

28 ART GALLERY OF NEW SOUTH WALES

This much-loved institution plays a prominent and gregarious role in Sydney society. Blockbuster international touring exhibitions arrive regularly and there's an outstanding permanent collection of Australian art, including a substantial Indigenous section.

29 BONDI TO COOGEE CLIFFTOP WALK

The simply sensational 6km (4 mile) Bondi to Coogee Clifftop Walk leads south from Bondi Beach along the cliff tops to Coogee via Tamarama, Bronte and Clovelly, interweaving panoramic views, patrolled beaches, sea baths, waterside parks and plaques recounting local Aboriginal stories.

30 AUSTRALIAN MUSEUM

Under an ongoing process of modernisation, this museum, established just 40 years after the First Fleet dropped anchor, is doing a brilliant job of it. A standout is the Indigenous Australians section, covering Aboriginal history and spirituality, from Dreaming stories to videos of the Freedom Rides of the 1960s.

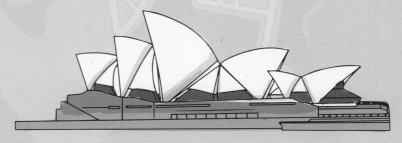

SOLUTIONS

San Francisco (Pages 6–9)

Vancouver (Pages 10–13)

New York (Pages 14–17)

Buenos Aires (Pages 18–19)

Rio (Pages 20–23)

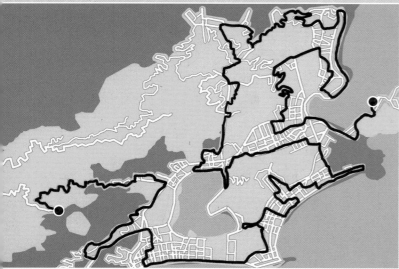

Lisbon (Pages 24–25)

Dublin (Pages 26–27)

London (Pages 28–31)

Barcelona (Pages 32–33)

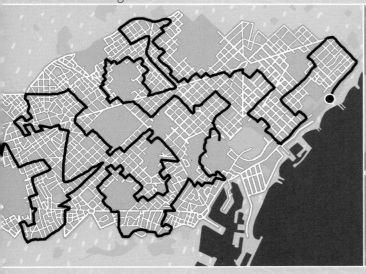

Paris (Pages 34–37)

Amsterdam (Pages 38–41)

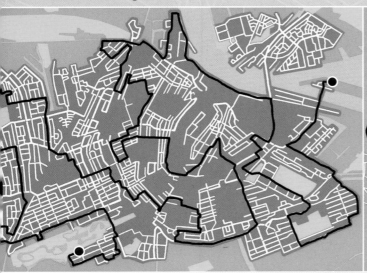

Rome (Pages 42–45)

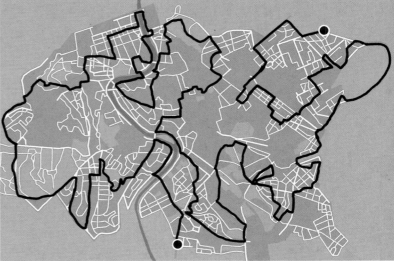

Copenhagen (Pages 46–47)

Berlin (Pages 48–51)

Prague (Pages 52–53)

Vienna (Pages 54–55)

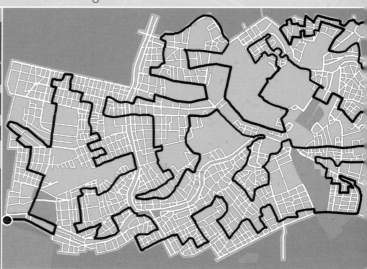

Stockholm (Pages 56–57)

Budapest (Pages 58–59)

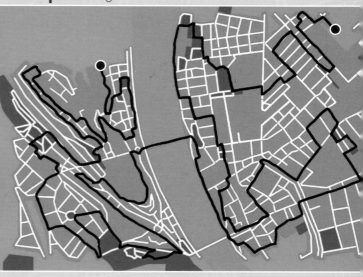

Kraków (Pages 60–61)

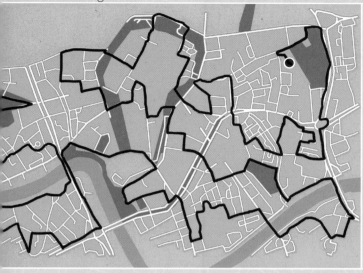

Athens (Pages 62–63)

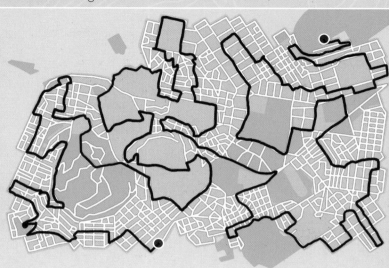

St Petersburg (Pages 64–65)

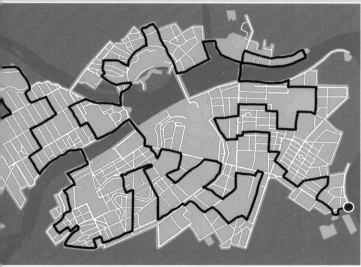

Marrakesh (Pages 66–67)

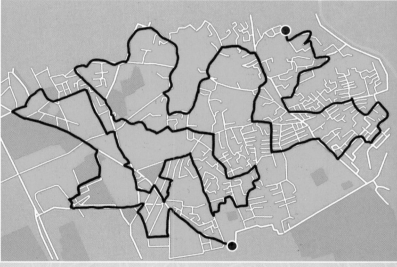

Cape Town (Pages 68–69)

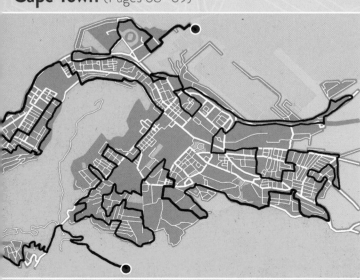

Dubai (Pages 70–71)

Delhi (Pages 72–73)

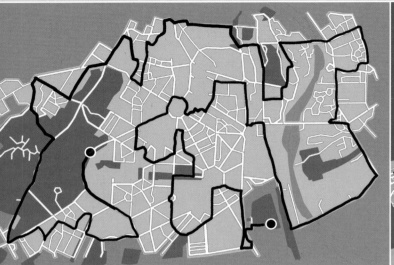

Hong Kong (Pages 74–77)

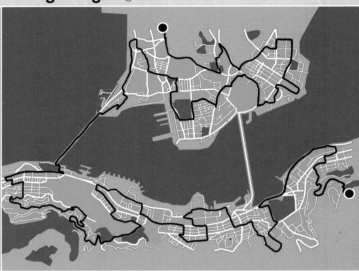

Běijïng (Pages 78–81)

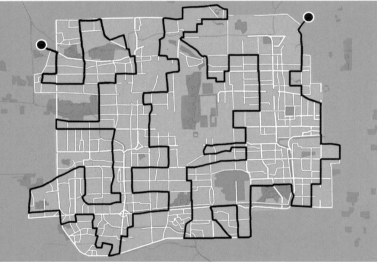

Seoul (Pages 82–85)

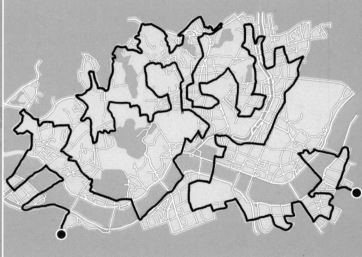

Kyoto (Pages 86–87)

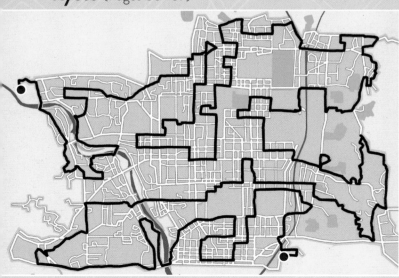

Sydney (Pages 88–91)

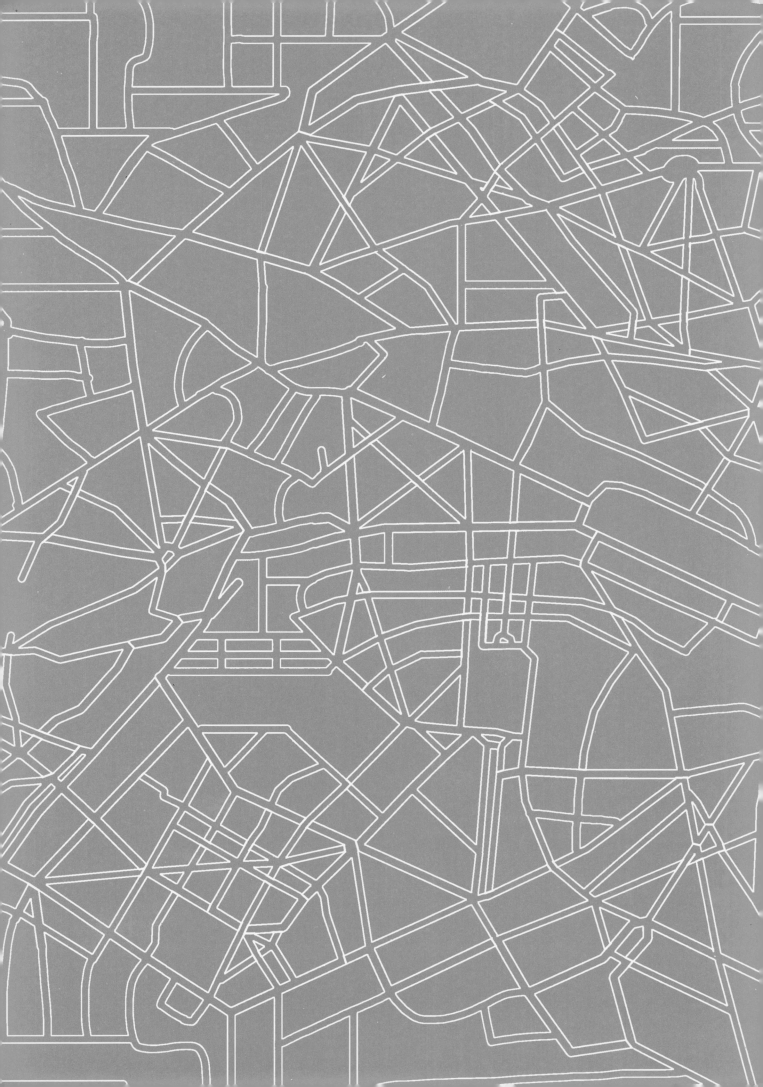